Biomass
Energy from Plants and Animals

Other books in the Fueling the Future series:

Biomass
Energy from Plants and Animals

Amanda de la Garza, *Book Editor*

Christine Nasso, *Publisher*
Elizabeth Des Chenes, *Managing Editor*

GREENHAVEN PRESS
A part of Gale, Cengage Learning

GALE
CENGAGE Learning

Detroit • New York • San Francisco • New Haven, Conn • Waterville, Maine • London

LIBRARY OF CONGRESS CATALOGING-IN-PUBLICATION DATA

Biomass: energy from plants and animals / Amanda de la Garza, book editor.
   p. cm. — (Fueling the future)
 Includes bibliographical references and index.
  ISBN 0-7377-3586-4 (lib. : alk. paper)
 1. Biomass energy. 2. Biomass energy industries—Cost effectiveness. 3. Global warming—Prevention. I. De la Garza, Amanda.
  TP339.B5646 2007
  333.95'39—dc22

                                     2006024557

Contents

Chapter 1: The Development of Biomass as an Energy Source

Chapter 2: Debates over Biomass

Chapter 3: The Future of Biomass Energy

Foreword

The wind farm at Altamont Pass in Northern California epitomizes many people's idea of wind power: Hundreds of towering white turbines generate electricity to power homes, factories, and businesses. The spinning turbine blades call up visions of a brighter future in which clean, renewable energy sources replace dwindling and polluting fossil fuels. The blades also kill over a thousand birds of prey each year. Every energy source, it seems, has its price.

The bird deaths at Altamont Pass make clear an unfortunate fact about all energy sources, including renewables: They have downsides. People want clean, abundant energy to power their modern lifestyles, but few want to pay the costs associated with energy production and use. Oil, coal, and natural gas contain high amounts of energy, but using them produces pollution. Commercial solar energy facilities require hundreds of acres of land and thus must be located in rural areas. Expensive and ugly transmission lines must then be run from the solar plants to the cities that need power. Producing hydrogen for fuel involves the use of dirty fossil fuels, tapping geothermal energy depletes ground water, and growing biomass for fuel ties up land that could be used to grow food. Hydroelectric power has become increasingly unpopular because dams flood vital habitats and kill wildlife and plants. Perhaps most controversial, nuclear power plants produce highly dangerous radioactive waste. People's reluctance to pay these environmental costs can be seen in the results of a 2006 Center for Economic and Civic Opinion poll. When asked how much they would support a power plant in their neighborhood, 66 percent of respondents said they would oppose it.

Many scientists warn that fossil fuel use creates emissions that threaten human health and cause global warming. Moreover, numerous scientists claim that fossil fuels are running out. As a result of these concerns, many nations have begun to revisit the energy sources that first powered human enterprises. In his 2006 State of the Union speech, U.S. President George W. Bush announced that since 2001 the United States has spent "$10 billion to develop cleaner, cheaper, and more reliable alternative energy sources," such as biomass and wind power. Despite Bush's positive rhetoric, many critics contend that the renewable energy sources he refers to are still as inefficient as they ever were and cannot possibly power modern economies. As Jerry Taylor and Peter Van Doren of the Cato Institute note, "The market share for non-hydro renewable energy . . . has languished between 1 and 3 percent for decades." Controversies such as this have been a constant throughout the history of humanity's search for the perfect energy source.

Greenhaven Press's Fueling the Future series explores this history. Each volume in the series traces the development of one energy source, and investigates the controversies surrounding its environmental impact and its potential to power humanity's future. The anthologies provide a variety of selections written by scientists, environmental activists, industry leaders, and government experts. Volumes also contain useful research tools, including an introductory essay providing important context, and an annotated table of contents that enables students to locate selections of interest easily. In addition, each volume includes an index, chronology, bibliography, glossary, and a Facts About section, which lists useful information about each energy source. Other features include numerous charts, graphs, and cartoons, which offer additional avenues for learning important information about the topic.

Fueling the Future volumes provide students with important resources for learning about the energy sources upon which human societies depend. Although it is easy to take energy for granted in developed nations, this series emphasizes how energy sources are also problematic. The U.S. Energy Information Administration calls energy "essential to life." Whether scientists will be able to develop the energy sources necessary to sustain modern life is the vital question explored in Greenhaven Press's Fueling the Future series.

Introduction

Keeping America competitive requires affordable energy. And here we have a serious problem: America is addicted to oil, which is often imported from unstable parts of the world. The best way to break this addiction is through technology.

—U.S. President George W. Bush, State of the Union Address, January 2006

It looks like alternative energy technology will be more expensive for a long time. Even if oil prices keep going higher, the alternatives won't be competitive for a while yet. Most of our current policy decisions are made to better utilize fossil fuels, rather than develop energy technology.

—Kei Koizumi, American Association for the Advancement of Science, *Oakland Tribune*, February 25, 2006

When energy experts talk about biomass, they mean organic matter that can be used to produce energy to heat homes, power automobiles, or produce electricity. Wood, for example, is a kind of biomass burned in fireplaces and campfires to produce heat and to cook food. Corn can be distilled into ethanol, which is used in combination with gasoline to run vehicles. The gas collected as organic matter decays in landfills can be used to produce electricity. Biomass is plentiful and renewable, making it appear the perfect energy source. However, energy experts are engaged in an intense debate over biomass. The controversy centers on two points: one, whether using biomass is wise, given the relative inefficiency of the technology that currently exists to break down biomass into a usable form; and two, whether growing biomass to be used as energy will exacerbate food shortages and environmental damage. Settling the debate over biomass appears more and more urgent as concerns over oil dependence and global warming grow.

The Search for Alternative Energy Sources Grows More Urgent

Concerns over oil dependence and global warming have led scientists and policy makers to explore the viability of alternative energy sources such as biomass. Although coal, oil, and natural gas continue to provide the vast majority of America's energy needs, many scientists believe that the burning of fossil fuels produces greenhouse gases that contribute to global warming. Numerous policy makers also contend that depending entirely on fossil fuels, which are finite resources, is unwise. Eventually, supplies will decrease, causing prices to soar, they claim. These experts, along with those concerned about global warming, recommend a transition to clean, renewable energy sources.

The crew of an ethanol-fueled race car prepares to run in the Indianapolis 500. Ethanol is a popular biomass fuel.

Heeding the call to explore alternatives, some scientists and policy makers have focused their attentions on biomass. Many experts believe that biomass could replace fossil fuels more quickly than could any other alternative because of the simplicity of biomass technology. For example, it is much simpler to burn grasses to produce electricity than it is to make electricity by building a nuclear power plant. In 2005 federal biomass research funding in the United States topped the list for alternative energy research funding. Yet in 2006 U.S. president George W. Bush cut that funding by 50 percent, suggesting that the government is reconsidering the viability of biomass as an energy source.

The Drawbacks of Using Biomass as an Energy Source

One of the major drawbacks of biomass has to do with economics. Developed nations such as the United States have built their modern economies on fossil fuels because these energy sources are economical. For example, electricity produced by a coal-burning plant is far cheaper than is electricity produced by a solar power plant. Because of this long-term reliance on fossil fuels, these nations' energy infrastructures—plants, pipelines, transmission lines, and filling stations—have been built around the use of coal, natural gas, and oil. Transitioning to alternative energy sources would require massive changes to the energy infrastructure, which would be costly to society. Individuals concerned about the burning of fossil fuels often find that they cannot afford to use alternative fuels. Installing solar panels on a house, for example, can cost a homeowner around fifteen thousand dollars, and buying a gas-electric hybrid car can cost a consumer several thousand dollars more than purchasing an equivalent standard model.

Biomass is not exempt from these economic realities. Societies may not want to invest in biomass-burning plants when they already have sufficient coal-burning plants in existence, for instance. Consumers may not wish to pay more for a car that burns ethanol. Municipal solid waste departments may not think it wise to install gas-collecting technologies on their landfills, fearing that the cost of installation will prove to be higher than the revenue earned from collecting the gas.

This new ethanol plant in Colorado is ready to turn corn into fuel.

Another concern is the fear that growing crops specifically for fuel will take food away from hungry people. Some experts believe that the already dire hunger problem in many parts of the world would worsen if more farmers started to replace their food crops with energy crops. Not everyone agrees that growing biomass for energy would exacerbate world hunger, however. Many commentators argue that poor rural areas would benefit by planting otherwise unusable land with crops to feed a biomass energy industry. The money they earned, these analysts maintain, could be used to purchase more nutritious food. Despite these assurances, the concern about hunger has dampened enthusiasm for biomass energy.

Environmental Concerns

Moreover, numerous environmental organizations argue that mainstreaming the use of biomass for energy worldwide would

Magic Johnson and Kermit the Frog introduce a new hybrid-fuel vehicle at a Chicago auto show. More biofuel cars will mean increased biomass crop production.

lead to dangerous reductions in biodiversity. They believe that landowners would be encouraged to plant massive tracts of one or two plant species that researchers deem especially suitable for conversion to energy. For instance, farmers all over the American Midwest might all plant saw grass on their land, creating monocultures. Monocultures do not have the balance and health of natural ecosystems, which comprise many kinds of naturally occurring species. This variety is crucial to ecosystem health. For example, insects usually eat just one or two types of plants. Thus, if the ecosystem contains numerous plant species, an invasion of any one type of insect would not completely destroy the whole system. In contrast, monocultures are susceptible to widespread damage by pests or disease unless farmers use large quantities of pesticides, fertilizers, and other chemicals. If a farmer plants only saw grass and an invasion of a saw grass–eating insect occurs, the whole crop is destroyed.

Environmentalists also worry that nations producing large amounts of biomass for fuel would put their natural resources at risk. Already in such countries as Indonesia and Malaysia, virgin rainforests are being felled to clear land for the production of palm and soya oil, which is processed into biofuels. Increasing American and European demand for biofuels could mean that developing countries will become main suppliers for the biomass industry. In this scenario, poorer nations would provide the land and cheap labor, but they also would sustain the potentially devastating environmental effects of massive fuel crop plantations.

Steam rises from a sugar cane–fueled ethanol plant in Brazil, one of many countries that could benefit from the use of renewable natural resources for fuel.

Many analysts point out, however, that supplier nations would also reap large financial benefits, which could help to offset the negative impacts of growing biomass for energy. These experts claim that when nations grow richer, they invest more in environmental protections. These protections can mitigate the environmental damage that occurs as a result of economic development.

Solving Problems with Technology

Many scientists say that technology can solve these environmental and economic problems. For instance, biomass energy researchers are developing technology that uses genetically engineered microorganisms to break down the tough cellulose of plant cells easily and quickly to produce ethanol. Developed by Lonnie Ingram, a microbiologist with the University of Florida's Institute of Food and Agricultural Sciences, one of these microorganisms produces a high yield of ethanol from biomass such as forestry and wood wastes, sugarcane residues, rice hulls, and other organic materials. "Until we developed this new technology, the chemical makeup of biomass prevented it from being used to make ethanol economically," Ingram said in a 2005 interview with the *University of Florida News*. Although other experts differ, he believes that more than 1 billion tons of biomass can be produced on a sustainable basis each year in the United States. Converting this to ethanol, the scientist contends, could replace 50 percent of all petroleum imported into the country.

Whether or not such an advance could help bring an end to society's reliance on fossil fuels remains to be seen. To be sure, people have long put their faith in technology to solve countless problems, often with disappointing results. On the other hand, some technological developments—for example, the scrubbers installed in the smokestacks of coal-fired plants, which have reduced dangerous emissions—have produced immense benefits. In any event, with more research dollars now being funneled to scientists exploring other energy sources, development of biomass technology may slow. However, because biomass is abundant and renewable, many scientists, activists, and policy makers are sure to continue believing in its potential to wean the world off of fossil fuels and reduce global warming.

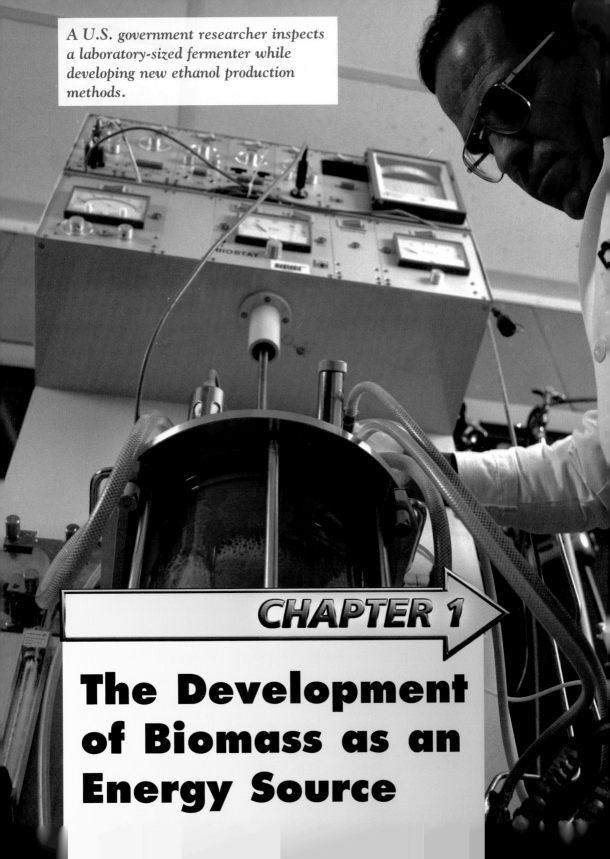

A U.S. government researcher inspects a laboratory-sized fermenter while developing new ethanol production methods.

CHAPTER 1

The Development of Biomass as an Energy Source

Fire: The First Use of Biomass

Norm Kidder

The burning of wood is the earliest use of biomass energy. In this selection Norm Kidder lists the various uses to which fire has been put. He emphasizes the central role of biomass in people's lives from the earliest times until the Industrial Revolution. Fire still plays a crucial role in the day-to-day lives of many in the developing world. Norm Kidder is one of the founders of and a contributor to *Primitive Ways*, a publication of the Idaho-based Society of Primitive Technology. This nonprofit organization is dedicated to the preservation of, research into, and teaching of primitive technology.

Landscape modification
Coppicing basket materials
Clearing brush for ease of travel and hunting
Removing thatch in late fall to promote wildflower seeds and bulbs for food
Burning meadows in summer to promote seed bearing grasses (weeding and fertilizing)
General burning to revitalize plant communities for greater abundance
Clear ground for food gathering

Hunting
Drive grasshoppers into cooking pit
Drive ground squirrels from holes
Smoke bees from hive

Norm Kidder, "Some Uses of Fire," *The Bulletin of Primitive Technology*, 2001.

Chase bison and other game over cliff or into trap
Night fishing with torch

Cooking
Roasting on coals or grill
Baking in pit or stone oven
Indirect cooking—as planking salmon
Boiling in clay pot or stone boiling in basket or wooden bowl,
    etc.
Parching seeds

An African baker removes a sheet of freshly baked bread
from his stone oven. Cooking with fire is one form of
biomass energy use.

Steam bending wood
  Straighten arrow, dart and spear shafts
  Recurve and reflex bows
  Bend basket rim sticks
  Bend looped stirring sticks for stone boiling
  Straighten hand drills for fire making

Smoking hides and meat to preserve

Softening tar and pitch for adhesive

Heat treating stone for tools

Early Native Americans used biomass energy when they burned logs and scooped out the charred wood to form dugout canoes.

Woodworking
Burn bowls and spoons
Dugout canoes
Burning down trees
Sharpening and fire hardening digging sticks and spears
General burn and scrape shaping

Making charcoal
For cooking and heating
For smelting metals
For firing pottery
For blacksmithing and metal casting
For pigment
For medicine and water purification

Charring to preserve house posts from insects and rot

Smudge fires to repel mosquitoes

Fire to repel predators

Heating shelters, etc.

Lighting (torches)

Smoking tobacco and medicines

Cauterizing wounds

Communication—signaling

Steaming
   To extract agave fibers
   To soften bone and wood for working

Ceremonies

How Biomass Energy Works

The Union of Concerned Scientists

In the following selection the Union of Concerned Scientists explains what biomass is and how it is used to supply various energy needs. As the organization describes, biomass consists of animal and plant wastes that can be used to create energy for heating homes and businesses and powering automobiles. For example, grasses can be burned to produce heat, and the methane gas produced by the decomposition of organic matter in landfills can be used as an energy source. Some biomass sources are specifically grown for use as energy while others are natural by-products of industrial and agricultural processes. Established in 1969, the Union of Concerned Scientists is a nonprofit partnership of scientists and citizens that conducts scientific analysis, helps develop policies, and works to educate citizens to achieve practical environmental solutions.

To many people, the most familiar forms of renewable energy are the wind and the sun. But biomass, energy from plants and animals, supplies almost 30 times as much energy in the United States as wind and solar power combined—and has the potential to supply much more.

What Is Biomass?
The term biomass refers to plant materials and animal wastes used for energy, especially tree and grass crops, and forestry, agricultural, and urban wastes. It is the oldest source of renewable

The Union of Concerned Scientists, "How Biomass Energy Works," www.ucsusa.org, December 5, 2005. Reproduced by permission.

energy known to humans, used since our ancestors learned the secret of fire.

Biomass is a renewable energy source because the energy it contains comes from the sun. Through the process of photosynthesis, chlorophyll in plants captures the sun's energy by converting carbon dioxide from the air and water from the ground into carbohydrates, complex compounds composed of carbon, hydrogen, and oxygen. When these carbohydrates are burned, they turn back into carbon dioxide and water and release the sun's energy they contain. In this way, biomass functions as a sort of natural battery for storing solar energy. As long as biomass is produced sustainably—with only as much used as is grown—the battery will last indefinitely.

A blazing, wood-burning fire is the oldest form of biomass energy.

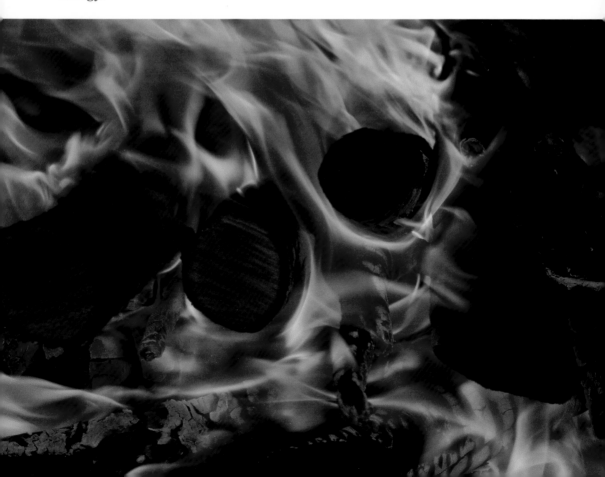

From the time of Prometheus [the titan who stole fire from the sun and gave it to humankind, according to Greek myth] to the present, the most common way to capture the energy from biomass was to burn it, to make heat, steam, and electricity. But advances in recent years have shown that there are more efficient and cleaner ways to use biomass. It can be converted into

A farmer examines his willow-tree crop, which can be chopped down while stimulating regrowth for repeated harvests.

liquid fuels, for example, or cooked in a process called "gasification" to produce combustible gases. And certain crops, like switchgrass and willow trees, are especially suited as "energy crops," plants grown specifically for energy.

Energy farms could supply a significant portion of America's energy needs, while at the same time revitalizing rural economies, providing energy independence and security, and achieving important environmental benefits. Rural communities of the future could be entirely self-sufficient when it comes to energy, using locally grown crops and residues to make fuels for their cars and tractors, and to generate heat and electricity for their homes.

Types of Biomass

There are many types of plants in the world, and many ways they can be used for energy production. In general there are two approaches: growing plants specifically for energy use, and using the residues from plants that are used for other things. The best approaches vary from region to region according to climate, soils, geography, population, and so on.

Energy Crops

Energy crops, also called "power crops," could be grown on farms in potentially very large quantities, just like food crops. Trees and grasses are the best crops for energy, but other, less agriculturally sustainable crops, like corn, tend to be used for energy purposes at present.

Trees. In addition to growing very fast, some trees will grow after being cut off close to the ground, a feature called "coppicing." Coppicing allows trees to be harvested every three to eight years for 20 or 30 years before replanting. These "short-rotation woody crops" grow as much as 40 feet high in the years between harvests. In the cooler, wetter regions of the northern United States, varieties of poplar, maple, black locust, and willow are the best choice. In the warmer Southeast, sycamore and sweetgum are best, while in the warmest parts of Florida and California, eucalyptus is likely to grow well.

Grasses. Thin-stemmed perennial grasses used to blanket the prairies, before the settlers replaced them with corn and beans. Switchgrass, big bluestem, and other native varieties grow quickly in many parts of the country, and can be harvested for up to 10 years before replanting. Thick-stemmed perennials, like sugar cane and elephant grass, can be grown in hot and wet climates like those of Florida and Hawaii.

Other crops. A third type of grass includes annuals commonly grown for food, such as corn and sorghum. Since these must be replanted every year, they require much closer management and greater use of fertilizers, pesticides, and energy. While corn currently provides most of the liquid fuel from biomass in the United States, there are more sustainable ways to produce energy from plants.

Oil plants. Plants such as soybeans and sunflowers produce oil, which can be used to make fuels. Like corn, though, these crops require intensive management and may not be sustainable in the longer term. A rather different type of oil crop with great promise for the future is microalgae. These tiny aquatic plants have the potential to grow extremely fast in the hot, shallow, saline water found in some lakes in the desert Southwest.

Biomass Residues

After plants have been used for other purposes, the leftover wastes can be used for energy. The forestry, agricultural, and manufacturing industries generate plant and animal wastes in large quantities. City waste, in the form of garbage and sewage, is also a source for biomass energy.

Forestry. Forestry wastes are the largest source of heat and electricity now, since lumber, pulp, and paper mills use them to power their factories. One large source of wood waste is tree tops and branches normally left behind in the forest after timber-harvesting operations. Some of these must be left behind to recycle necessary nutrients to the forest and to provide habitat for birds and mammals, but some could be collected sustainably. Other sources of wood waste are sawdust and bark from sawmills, shavings produced during the manufacture of furniture, and organic sludge, or "liquor," from pulp and paper mills.

Different Types of Biomass

Energy Crops

Plants grown specifically for energy use

Trees

Examples: willow, sweetgum, poplar

Grasses

Examples: sugar cane, switchgrass

Crops

Examples: corn, sorghum, wheat

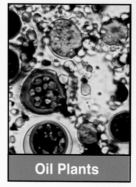

Oil Plants

Examples: microalgae, soybeans, sunflowers

Waste Matter

Leftover residue from plants that are used for other things

Forestry

Examples: lumber scrap, sawdust, paper mill sludge

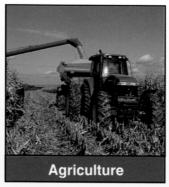

Agriculture

Examples: waste from harvested crops, manure

Cities

Examples: leftover wood, garbage, landfill gas

Agriculture. Just as in forestry, most crop residues are left in the field. Some should be left there to maintain cover against erosion and to recycle nutrients, but some could be collected for fuel. Animal farms produce many "wet wastes" in the form of manure. These wastes are commonly spread on fields, not just for their nutrient value, but for disposal. Runoff from overfertilization threatens rural lakes and streams and can contaminate drinking water. Processing crops into food also produces many usable wastes.

Cities. People generate biomass wastes in many forms, including "urban wood waste" (like shipping pallets and leftover construction wood), the biomass portion of garbage (paper, food, leather, yardwaste, etc.) and the gas given off by landfills when biomass waste decomposes. Even our sewage can be used as energy; some sewage treatment plants capture the methane given off by sewage and burn it for heat and power. This reduces air pollution, emissions of global warming gases, and nuisance odors, while producing useful energy.

Converting Biomass to Energy

The old way of converting biomass to energy, practiced for thousands of years, is simply to burn it to produce heat. This is still the use to which most biomass is put, in the United States and elsewhere. The heat can be used directly, for heating, cooking, and industrial processes, or indirectly, to produce electricity. The problems with burning biomass are that much of the energy is wasted and that it can cause some pollution if it is not carefully controlled.

An approach that may increase the use of biomass energy in the short term is to burn it mixed with coal in power plants. Utilities in New York and Wisconsin are experimenting with this approach as a way to reduce carbon dioxide emissions.

A number of noncombustion methods for converting biomass to energy have one thing in common—they convert raw biomass into a variety of gaseous, liquid, or solid fuels before using it. The carbohydrates in biomass, which are compounds of oxygen, carbon, and hydrogen, can be broken down into a variety of chemicals, some of which are useful fuels. This conversion can be done in three ways:

- *Thermochemical.* When plant matter is heated, but not burned, it breaks down into various gases, liquids, and solids. These products can then be processed into gas and liquid fuels like methane and alcohol. Biomass gasifiers capture methane released from the plants and burn it in a gas turbine to produce electricity. Another approach is to take these fuels and run them through fuel cells, converting the hydrogen-rich fuels into electricity and water, with few or no emissions.

- *Biochemical.* Bacteria, yeasts, and enzymes also break down carbohydrates. Fermentation, the process used to make wine, changes biomass liquids into alcohol, which is inflammable. A similar process is used to turn corn into grain alcohol or ethanol, which is mixed with gasoline to make gasohol. Also, when bacteria break down biomass, methane and carbon dioxide are produced. This methane can be captured, in sewage treatment plants and landfills, for example, and burned for heat and power.
- *Chemical.* Biomass oils, like soybean and canola oil, can be chemically converted into a liquid fuel similar to diesel fuel, and into gasoline additives. Cooking oil from restaurants, for example, has been used as a source to make "biodiesel" for trucks. (A better way to produce biodiesel is to use algae as a source of oils.) Biomass is also used to make gas additives like ETBE and MTBE, which reduce air emissions from cars.

Myths About Biomass

One persistent myth about biomass is that it takes more energy to produce fuels from biomass than the fuels themselves contain. In other words, that it is a net energy loser. In fact, current ethanol production uses corn, one of the most energy-intensive crops, and then uses just the kernels from the corn plant, and not even the entire kernel. Even so, this process yields 50 percent more energy than it takes to make the ethanol, so it is a net gainer.

Nonetheless, we could do much better. By making ethanol from energy crops, we could obtain between four and five times the energy that we put in, and by making electricity we could get perhaps 10 times or more. In the future, to make a truly sustainable biomass energy system, we would have to replace fossil fuels

A Brooklyn man pumps discarded vegetable oil from a restaurant into his biodiesel-fueled truck.

with biomass or other renewable fuels to plant and harvest the crops.

Another important consideration with biomass energy systems is that biomass contains less energy per pound than fossil fuels. This means that raw biomass typically can't be cost-effectively shipped more than about 50 miles before it is converted into fuel or energy. It also means that biomass energy systems are likely to be smaller than their fossil fuel counterparts, because it is hard to gather and process more than this quantity of fuel in one place. This has the advantage that local, rural communities—and perhaps even individual farms—will be able to design energy systems that are self-sufficient, sustainable, and perfectly adapted to their own needs.

The Rise and Fall of California's Biomass Industry

Gregory Morris

In this selection Gregory Morris examines the explosive growth of California's biomass industry during the 1980s in response to a national energy crisis. As oil prices skyrocketed, the state turned to renewables such as biomass for its energy. As a result, California became a world leader in the use of biomass energy. However, when oil and gas prices dropped dramatically in the 1990s, many biomass-powered plants shut down. Biomass energy, which suddenly became far more costly than oil and gas, could no longer compete with other energy sources. California still has many operating biomass plants, but the future of the industry is uncertain, Morris claims. Gregory Morris, a member of the Pacific Institute for Studies in Development, Environment, and Security, wrote this report under contract to the National Renewable Energy Laboratory (NREL). The NREL is the nation's primary laboratory for research and development in renewable energy and energy efficiency.

California has the largest and most diverse biomass energy industry in the world. At its peak the California biomass energy industry produced almost 4.5 billion kWhs [kilowatthours] per year of electricity, and provided a beneficial use outlet for more than 10 million tons per year of the state's solid wastes. The peak, however, occurred during the early 1990s.

Gregory Morris, "Biomass Energy Production in California: The Case for a Biomass Policy Initiative," www.nrel.gov, November 2000. Reproduced by permission.

Since that time a quarter of the biomass energy facilities have agreed to buyouts of their power sales contracts and terminated operations, while others have reduced their operations. This has occurred because of concerns about the long-term viability of these facilities in a competitive, deregulated electricity market. This uncertainty casts an ominous cloud over the future viability of biomass energy generation in California.

California's Leadership

California has a diversity and extent of agriculture and forestry unrivaled in the world. Both activities produce large quantities of solid wastes, many of which are biomass residues that can be used as fuel. Before the federal Public Utilities Regulatory Policy Act (PURPA) was passed in 1978 only a few biomass-fired boilers were operating in California, and little electricity was being generated from biomass. Most of the state's biomass wastes were being disposed of, mainly by open burning and landfill burial. PURPA changed all that by requiring that electric utility companies buy privately produced power at their "avoided cost" of generation. PURPA created the market context that allowed for the development of the independent power industry in the United States. High avoided cost rates in many areas of the country, and favorable federal tax treatment for investments in renewable energy projects, provided the motivation for its development.

California was a leader in the development of renewable energy generating facilities. A combination of circumstances, including a high growth rate in electricity demand, oil dependence, and rising concerns about environmental deterioration led to the implementation of state energy policies that were highly conducive to the development of renewable energy sources. These policies and opportunities stimulated a major development of biomass energy generating capacity in the state. During a period of less than 15 years (roughly 1980–1993) nearly 1,000 MW [megawatts] of biomass generating capacity were placed into service. The biomass energy sector expanded from an outlet for a small quantity of the state's wood processing residues, to an essential component of the state's solid-waste disposal infrastructure. Today the California biomass energy industry provides a beneficial use for almost 6.5 million tons of the state's solid wastes. However, it has a highly uncertain future. The expiration of fixed-price power sales provisions for many facilities, combined with the deregulation of the electric utility industry and the current availability of cheap natural gas, threatens its long-term economic viability.

A lumber mill slices logs into planks in California, a state with many forests and a leader in the use of biomass as a power source.

The 1980s: A Decade of Growth

The early 1980s mark the nascent period for the California biomass energy industry. During this period several pioneering biomass energy generating facilities were built and placed into service. The early facilities tended to be small, generally 2–10 MW, and most were associated with sawmills or food processing operations that were looking for beneficial use outlets for their wastes. . . .

Also during the early 1980s, the California electric utility companies developed standard offer contracts for power purchases from independent generators. These contracts had particularly favorable provisions for renewable energy projects. A great deal of biomass project development activity was initiated during this period, which led to an explosion of new facility openings during the second half of the decade.

The Rise and Fall of California's Biomass Operating Capacity

Operating Capacity (in Megawatts)

900 — 800 — 700 — 600 — 500 — 400 — 300 — 200 — 100 — 0

1980 1981 1982 1983 1984 1985 1986 1987 1988 1989 1990 1991 1992 1993 1994 1995 1996 1997 1998 1999 2000

Year

Source: Energy Information Administration, U.S. Department of Energy, 2005 (www.eia.doe.gov).

The California biomass energy industry became an important part of the state's electricity supply infrastructure, and its waste disposal infrastructures during the second half of the 1980s. The incentives for renewable energy development that were offered during the first half of the decade led to the opening of 33 new biomass generating facilities between 1985 and 1990. A few of the pioneering facilities were shut down during this period, but the state's total operating biomass energy capacity grew by more than 650 MW. The average size of the facilities brought on line during this period was about 17.5 MW; the largest facilities were 50 MW. The explosive growth of biomass generating capacity culminated in 1990, when 11 new facilities were commissioned in a single year, adding 232 MW of biomass generating capacity to the state's electricity supply. . . .

The second half of the 1980s was also significant for a reversal in world oil markets. World oil prices, which had remained high since the price explosions of the 1970s, collapsed during the period 1985–1986. . . .

The attention of the biomass generating facilities focused on . . . a looming crisis in the biomass fuels market. As the state's installed biomass generating capacity grew rapidly during the latter half of the 1980s, the demand for fuel soon overwhelmed the readily available supply. Virtually all sawmill and food processing residues that did not have higher valued uses were being sold into the fuel market, and still there was a significant deficit between biomass supply and demand. Numerous efforts were under way to develop technologies to produce biomass fuels from new sources of supply, such as agricultural prunings, agricultural field residues, forestry residues, and urban waste wood, with rising fuel prices providing the incentive. The state's biomass fuels crisis peaked in 1990 with average prices topping $40/bdt [bone-dry ton] of fuel, and spot prices reaching $60/bdt or higher. Moreover, several major new facilities were approaching the completion of construction, and there was a fear that biomass fuel prices might continue to rise.

The 1990s: Maturity and Consolidation

At the end of 1990 more than 770 MW of biomass energy generating capacity were operating in California, and an additional 100

MW of capacity were in advanced stages of construction. The early years of the 1990s saw the state's biomass energy industry stabilize at a level of about 750 MW of operating capacity. . . .

The California biomass fuels market also stabilized during the early 1990s, with average market prices settling at a level of about $37.50/bdt, at an average consumption level of approximately 9 million tons per year. This stability was reached despite the beginning, in 1990, of a long-term decline in the state's wood products industry, which was caused by a combination of environmental restrictions and economic conditions. This is significant because wood processing residues are the lowest-cost biomass fuels in the state. By the end of 1993 the biomass energy industry appeared to have attained a level of maturity, and a workable equilibrium between fuel supply and fuel demand had been established. Although there were winners and losers, the California biomass energy industry as a whole successfully weathered the storm of the fuel crisis that marked the beginning of the decade.

How the *Blue Book* Doomed the Biomass Industry

The stability, however, was short lived. In April 1994 the California Public Utilities Commission (CPUC) issued its landmark *Blue Book* proposal for restructuring the state's regulated electric utility industry. The *Blue Book* proposal provided for competition among generating sources on the basis of price alone, without regard to non-market factors such as resource diversity and environmental impact. This represented a major threat to biomass energy generation. Because of the low density of biomass fuels and the resultant high handling and transportation costs, the relatively small size of biomass generating facilities, and the low cost of natural gas, the cost of power production from biomass was inherently higher than the cost of power generation using natural gas. Competition based on price factors alone would not favor biomass energy generation. . . .

Over the next 3 years 17 biomass facilities, rated collectively at more than 215 MW, accepted buyout offers and shut down operations. Unlike in earlier years, when only marginal facilities

Conveyer belts transport huge piles of wood waste toward a generator at a biomass power plant in Anderson, California.

were closed, most of the facilities that shut down following the issuing of the *Blue Book* proposal were first-rate facilities that had been operating efficiently and profitably until the buyouts. . . .

Annual biomass fuel use in the state shrank by 37% during the 2 years following the appearance of the *Blue Book* proposal. More than 3 million tons/year of biomass residues that were being used for energy production in the early 1990s were returned to open burning and landfilling for disposal. In addition, at its peak the state's biomass industry was supporting forest treatment operations on approximately 60,000 acres/year of forest land that was not otherwise being commercially harvested or treated. These treatments reduce the risk of destructive wildfires and improve the health and productivity of the thinned forest. With the retraction in the demand for biomass fuels the amount of this type of forest treatment activity has declined dramatically.

The Development of California's Biomass Industry

California Biomass Power Plants, 1985

California Biomass Power Plants, 1990

California Biomass Power Plants, 1995

California Biomass Power Plants, 2000

Megawatts Produced
- 0–15
- 15–30
- 30–60

- Operating
- Idle
- Dismantled

Source: National Renewable Energy Laboratory, 2000 (www.nrel.gov).

The CPUC's original restructuring proposal underwent a process of refinement that lasted for more than 2 years. By the summer of 1996 the CPUC had acknowledged the desirability of incorporating environmental factors into the choice of energy sources, and embraced the concept of a minimum purchase requirement for renewable energy sources. A working group made up of the utility companies, independent power generators, and public interest groups worked on formulating a consensus proposal to the CPUC to implement a minimum renewables purchase requirement for California's regulated electric utility sector. The biomass industry . . . played a key role in this process.

In late August 1996, just before the end of the state legislative session, the California legislature formulated its own electric utility restructuring program, superseding the efforts of the CPUC. The legislation that emerged, AB 1890, included a program of short-term support for renewable energy during the 4-year transition period (1998–2001) to full implementation of restructuring. However, no long-term support program for renewables was included. AB 1890 explicitly recognized the special waste disposal benefits associated with biomass energy in California. The legislation directed the California Environmental Protection Agency (Cal/EPA) to study policies that would shift some costs of biomass energy production away from the electric ratepayer, and onto the beneficiaries of the waste disposal services it provides. Cal/EPA was directed to report to the legislature on biomass cost-shifting measures by April 1997.

Cal/EPA had difficulty coming to grips with this political football. . . . The result was a watered-down report that provided the legislature with no basis for enacting the kinds of cost-shifting policies for biomass envisioned in AB 1890.

The legislature made one more attempt to develop the background necessary for the developing biomass support policies in California. In 1998, AB 2273 was passed and signed into law. AB 2273 directs Cal/EPA to report annually to the legislature on progress in developing biomass cost-shifting policies in the state. CIWMB [California Integrated Waste Management Board] was assigned the lead role in developing the first report under this legislation. Although a report was prepared in early

1999 and sent to the Cal/EPA Board for approval, it was never released and sent to the legislature.

Despite the cloud of uncertainty over the future viability of biomass energy production in California, the state's biomass energy industry operated with relative stability during the latter half of the 1990s. Following the shutdowns of 1994–1996, 27 biomass facilities, representing 540 MW of generating capacity, remained in operation. . . .

The operating biomass energy generating capacity in California actually increased slightly at the end of the 1990s, to almost 600 MW. This was mainly because two 25-MW facilities that had accepted contract buyouts and shut down operations in 1994 had special provisions in their buyouts that provided for restarting the facilities at the end of their fixed-price periods. These facilities resumed operations in 1998 and 1999, respectively. Biomass fuel use increased by 15% over its low point following the 1994–1996 shutdowns, but was still more than 30% lower than the peak level achieved during the early part of the decade.

A Brazilian truck driver fills his tank with palm-oil biodiesel.

CHAPTER 2

Debates over Biomass

Biomass Should Be Used to Produce Transportation Fuels

Oak Ridge National Laboratory

This press release from the Oak Ridge National Laboratory (ORNL) in Oak Ridge, Tennessee, summarizes a report it created at the request of the U.S. Department of Energy's Office of Energy Efficiency and Renewable Energy. The laboratory argues for increased U.S. investment in biomass technology. ORNL suggests that the United States could easily produce enough biomass to cut petroleum use by 30 percent. Moreover, the study's authors maintain that production of this quantity of biomass would not use up land needed to grow food. Using more biomass energy would increase national energy security, reduce greenhouse gas emissions by up to 10 percent, and provide jobs for workers in rural areas, ORNL claims.

The authors of this report are Bob Perlack, Lynn Wright, and Anthony Turhollow of the Oak Ridge National Laboratory, Bryce Stokes of the U.S. Department of Agriculture (USDA) Forest Service, and Don Erbach of the USDA Agriculture Research Service. The ORNL conducts research in basic and applied science to find creative solutions to complicated energy problems.

Relief from soaring prices at the gas pump could come in the form of corncobs, cornstalks, switchgrass and other types of biomass, according to a joint feasibility study for the departments of Agriculture and Energy.

Oak Ridge National Laboratory, "Growth in Biomass Could Put U.S. on Road to Energy Independence," www.ornl.gov, April 21, 2005. Reproduced by permission.

The recently completed Oak Ridge National Laboratory report outlines a national strategy in which 1 billion dry tons of biomass—any organic matter that is available on a renewable or recurring basis—would displace 30 percent of the nation's petroleum consumption for transportation. Supplying more than 3 percent of the nation's energy, biomass already has surpassed hydropower as the largest domestic source of renewable energy, and researchers believe much potential remains.

"Our report answers several key questions," said Bob Perlack, a member of ORNL's Environmental Sciences Division and a co-author of the report. "We wanted to know how large a role biomass could play, whether the United States has the land resources and whether such a plan would be economically viable."

Switchgrass (left) and corn (right) are two of the most popular biomass crops in the United States.

Looking at just forestland and agricultural land, the two largest potential biomass sources, the study found potential exceeding 1.3 billion dry tons per year. That amount is enough to produce biofuels to meet more than one-third of the current demand for transportation fuels, according to the report.

Such an amount, which would represent a six-fold increase in production from the amount of biomass produced today, could be achieved with only relatively modest changes in land use and agricultural and forestry practices.

"One of the main points of the report is that the United States can produce nearly 1 billion dry tons of biomass annually from agricultural lands and still continue to meet food, feed and export demands," said Robin Graham, leader for Ecosystem and Plant Sciences in ORNL's Environmental Sciences Division.

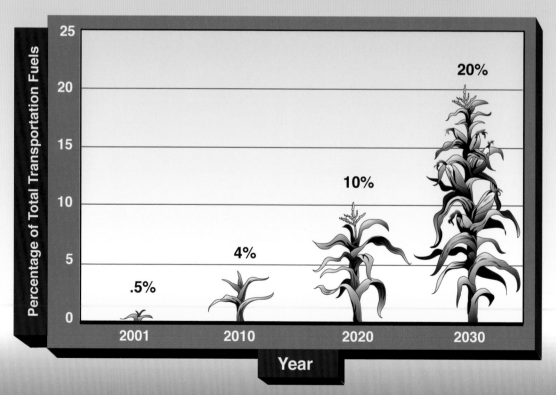

Source: Oak Ridge National Laboratory, 2005 (www.ornl.gov).

The benefits of an increased focus on biomass include increased energy security as the U.S. would become less dependent on foreign oil, a potential 10 percent reduction in greenhouse gas emissions and an improved rural economic picture.

Current production of ethanol is about 3.4 billion gallons per year, but that total could reach 80 billion gallons or more under the scenario outlined in this report. Such an increase in ethanol production would see transportation fuels from biomass increase from 0.5 percent of U.S. consumption in 2001 to 4 percent in 2010, 10 percent in 2020 and 20 percent in 2030. In fact, depending on several factors, biomass could supply 15 percent of the nation's energy by 2030.

Meanwhile, biomass consumption in the industrial sector would increase at an annual rate of 2 percent through 2030, while biomass consumption by electric utilities would double every 10 years through 2030. During the same time, production of chemicals and materials from bio-based products would increase from about 12.5 billion pounds, or 5 percent of the current production of target U.S. chemical commodities in 2001, to 12 percent in 2010, 18 percent in 2020 and 25 percent in 2030.

Nearly half of the 2,263 million acres that comprise the land base of the U.S. has potential for growing biomass. About 33 percent of the land area is classified as forest, 26 percent as grassland, 20 percent as cropland, 13 percent as urban areas, swamps and deserts, and 8 percent as special uses such as public facilities.

The report, titled "Biomass as Feedstock for a Bioenergy and Bioproducts Industry: The Technical Feasibility of a Billion-Ton Annual Supply," was sponsored by DOE's [Department of Energy's] Office of Energy Efficiency and Renewable Energy,

FACTS TO CONSIDER

The Military Backs Biofuels

Biodiesel use in the military is just beginning to take off. Earlier this year, the Department of the Navy ordered all Navy and Marine installations in the United States to begin using biodiesel when possible. Large naval bases such as the one at Norfolk, Virginia, are installing additional fuel tanks specifically for biodiesel. The Navy is even experimenting with brewing its own biodiesel from the used vegetable oil that comes out of its mess halls.

Dan Orzech, *Wired News*, September 28, 2005.

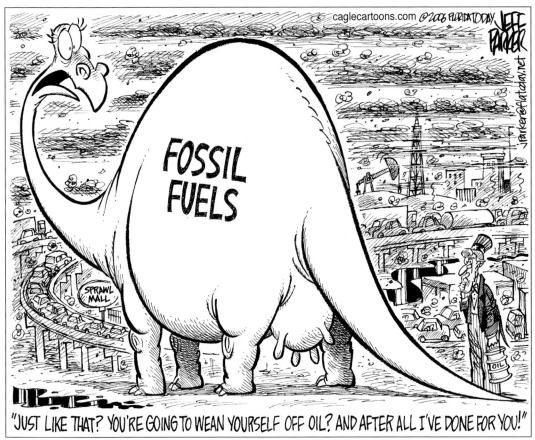

"JUST LIKE THAT? YOU'RE GOING TO WEAN YOURSELF OFF OIL? AND AFTER ALL I'VE DONE FOR YOU!"

Jeff Parker, *Florida Today*/Cagle Cartoons.

Office of Biomass Program. Lynn Wright and Anthony Turhollow of ORNL, Bryce Stokes of the USDA [U.S. Department of Agriculture] Forest Service and Don Erbach of the USDA Agriculture Research Service are co-authors of the report. The complete report is available at http:/feedstockreview.ornl.gov/pdf/billion_ton_vision.pdf.

Biomass Should Not Be Used to Produce Transportation Fuels

David Pimentel and Tad W. Patzek

Professors David Pimentel and Tad W. Patzek announce the result of their study on biofuels in the following selection. They say their study demonstrates that the process of transforming plants into fuels such as ethanol uses far more energy than it produces. Based on the study's findings, Pimentel and Patzek argue that using biomass to produce transportation fuels is not economically viable. David Pimentel is a professor of ecology and evolutionary biology at Cornell University. Tad W. Patzek works at the University of California–Berkeley as a professor of civil engineering.

The United States desperately needs a liquid fuel replacement for oil in the future. The use of oil is projected to peak about 2007 and the supply is then projected to be extremely limited in 40–50 years. Alternative liquid fuels from various sources have been sought for many years. Two panel studies by the U.S. Department of Energy (USDOE) concerned with ethanol production using corn and liquid fuels from biomass energy report a negative energy return. These reports were reviewed by 26 expert U.S. scientists independent of the USDOE: the findings indicated that the conversion of corn into ethanol energy was negative and these findings were unanimously approved.

David Pimentel and Tad W. Patzek, "Ethanol Production Using Corn, Switchgrass, and Wood; Biodiesel Using Soybean and Sunflower," *Natural Resources Research*, vol. 14, March 2005, pp. 65-75. Reproduced with kind permission from Springer Science and Business Media and the authors.

Numerous other investigations have confirmed these findings over the past two decades.

A review of the reports that indicate that corn ethanol production provides a positive return indicates that many inputs were omitted. It is disappointing that many of the inputs were omitted because this misleads U.S. policy makers and the public. . . .

Corporations and Politicians Clash with Science

The USDA [U.S. Department of Agriculture] claims that ethanol production provides a net energy return. In addition, some large corporations, including Archer Daniels Midland, support the production of ethanol using corn and are making huge profits from ethanol production, which is subsidized by federal and state governments. Some politicians also support the production of corn ethanol based on their mistaken belief that ethanol production provides large benefits for farmers, whereas in fact farmer profits are minimal. In contrast to the USDA, numerous scientific studies have concluded that ethanol production does not provide a net energy balance, that ethanol is not a renewable energy source, is not an economical fuel, and its production and use contribute to air, water, and soil pollution and global warming. Growing large amounts of corn necessary for ethanol production occupies cropland suitable for food production and raises serious ethical issues. . . .

The objective of this analysis is to update and assess all the recognized inputs that operate in the entire ethanol production system. These inputs include the direct costs in terms of energy and dollars for producing the corn feedstock as well as for the fermentation/distillation process. Additional costs to the consumer

How Ethanol Is Made

Most U.S. ethanol makers use yeast to ferment the starch and sugars in corn, much like the process used to make alcoholic beverages (such as beer) from fermented grains.

1 HARVEST

Corn is harvested and kernels are removed from cobs.

2 GRINDERS

Corn kernels are crushed to a fine powder in grinders.

3 MIXTURE

The cornmeal is mixed with water; enzymes and yeast are added to help fermentation. The mixture (called mash) is placed in large fermenting tanks.

4 FERMENTERS

The mash ferments for a few days. This process turns starch into sugar, and the sugar then turns to alcohol.

5 BOILERS

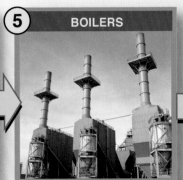

The solid corn mash is discarded and used as livestock feed. The remaining alcoholic liquid is pumped into boilers where it is heated.

6 DISTILLERS

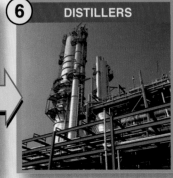

Water is removed by a process called distilling. The fermented liquid is boiled until steam rises and condenses in the still. Steam-water escapes or is drained off as waste.

7 SHIPPING & STORAGE

The remaining liquid is ethanol alcohol. It is stored in large tanks or shipped via tanker trucks and rail cars.

8 FUEL

In the U.S., ethanol is usually mixed with regular petroleum-based gasoline for use in today's cars.

Senator John McCain speaks out against federal subsidies that keep ethanol production costs down.

include federal and state subsidies, plus costs associated with environmental pollution and degradation that occur during the entire production system. Ethanol production in the United States does not benefit the nation's energy security, its agriculture, the economy, or the environment. Also, ethical questions are raised by diverting land and precious food into fuel and actually adding a net amount of pollution to the environment.

The conversion of corn and other food/feed crops into ethanol by fermentation is a well-known and established technology. The ethanol yield from a large production plant is about 1 l [liter] of ethanol from 2.69 kg [kilograms] of corn grain.

The production of corn in the United States requires a significant energy and dollar investment. For example, to produce average corn yield of 8,655 kg/ha [kilograms per hectare] of corn using average production technology requires the expenditure of about 8.1 million kcal [kilocalories] (about 271 gallons of gasoline equivalents/ha). The production costs are about $917/ha for the 8,655 kg or approximately 11¢/kg of corn produced. To produce a liter of ethanol requires 29% more fossil energy than is produced as ethanol and costs 42¢ per l ($1.59 per gallon). The corn feedstock alone requires nearly 50% of the energy input. . . .

Based on current ethanol production technology and recent oil prices, ethanol costs substantially more to produce in dollars than it is worth on the market. Clearly, without the more than $3 billion of federal and state government subsidies each year, U.S. ethanol production would be reduced or cease, confirming the basic fact that ethanol production is uneconomical. Senator [John] McCain reports that including the direct subsidies for ethanol plus the subsidies for corn grain, a liter costs 79¢ ($3/gallon). If the production costs of producing a liter of ethanol were added to the tax subsidies, then the total cost for a liter of ethanol would be $1.24. Because of the relatively low energy content of ethanol, 1.6 liters of ethanol have the energy equivalent of 1 liter of gasoline. Thus, the cost of producing an equivalent amount of ethanol to equal a liter of gasoline is $1.88 ($7.12 per gallon of gasoline), while the current [2005] cost of producing a liter of gasoline is 33¢.

Increasing the Use of Biofuels Will Lead to Mass Starvation

George Monbiot

Columnist George Monbiot argues in this selection that using biomass to produce fuels would cause widespread hunger. Because natural resources are finite, there is only so much land suitable for growing crops. Because people who want fuels to power their cars have more money than do people who desperately need food, land will inevitably be used to create biomass for fuels, not for growing food crops, he claims. Monbiot also argues that the destruction of more rain forest would certainly follow if financial interest in planting crops for biofuels continues to increase. George Monbiot is the author of *The Age of Consent: A Manifesto for a New World Order* and *Captive State: The Corporate Takeover of Britain*, as well as several investigative travel books. He also writes a weekly column for the *Guardian* newspaper.

I f human beings were without sin, we would still live in an imperfect world. Adam Smith's notion that by pursuing his own interest, a man "frequently promotes that of . . . society more effectually than when he really intends to promote it", and Karl Marx's picture of a society in which "the free development of each is the condition for the free development of all" are both mocked by one obvious constraint. The world is finite. This means that when one group of people pursues its own interests, it damages the interests of others.

George Monbiot, "Comment: Fuel for Nought," *The Guardian*, November 23, 2004. Copyright Guardian Newspapers Limited 2004. Reproduced by permission of the author.

It is hard to think of a better example than the current enthusiasm for biofuels. These are made from plant oils or crop wastes or wood, and can be used to run cars and buses and lorries [trucks]. Burning them simply returns to the atmosphere the carbon that the plants extracted while they were growing. So switching from fossil fuels to biodiesel and bioalcohol is now being promoted as the solution to climate change.

Excitement over Biofuels

Next month [December 2004], the British government will have to set a target for the amount of transport fuel that will come from crops. The European Union [EU] wants 2% of the

A Kansas congressman poses in an ethanol-powered truck, just one example of the various vehicles that run on biofuels.

Bright yellow flowers bloom atop the rapeseed (or canola) plant, the most productive fuel-oil crop in the United Kingdom.

oil we use to be biodiesel by the end of next year, rising to 6% by 2010 and 20% by 2020. To try to meet these targets, the government has reduced the tax on biofuels by 20p [approximately 40 cents in 2006] a litre while the EU is paying farmers an extra €45 [$80] a hectare to grow them.

Everyone seems happy about this. The farmers and the chemicals industry can develop new markets, the government can meet its commitments to cut carbon emissions, and environmentalists can celebrate the fact that plant fuels reduce local pollution as well as global warming. Unlike hydrogen fuel cells, biofuels can be deployed straightaway. This, in fact, was how Rudolf Diesel expected his invention to be used. When he demonstrated his engine at the World Exhibition in 1900, he ran it on peanut oil. "The use of vegetable oils for engine fuels may seem insignificant today," he predicted. "But such oils may become in course of time as important as petroleum." Some enthusiasts are predicting that if fossil fuel prices continue to rise, he will soon be proved right.

Biofuels Would Create a Global Humanitarian Disaster

I hope not. Those who have been promoting these fuels are well-intentioned, but wrong. They are wrong because the world is finite. If biofuels take off, they will cause a global humanitarian disaster.

Used as they are today, on a very small scale, they do no harm. A few thousand greens in the United Kingdom are running their cars on used chip [French fry] fat. But recycled cooking oils could supply only 100,000 tonnes of diesel a year in this country, equivalent to one 380th of our road transport fuel.

It might also be possible to turn crop wastes such as wheat stubble into alcohol for use in cars. . . . I'd like to see the figures, but I find it hard to believe that we will be able to extract more energy than we use in transporting and processing straw. But the EU's plans, like those of all the enthusiasts for biolocomotion, depend on growing crops specifically for fuel. As soon as you examine the implications, you discover that the cure is as bad as the disease.

Using Land for Fuel Crops Is Misguided

Road transport in the UK [United Kingdom] consumes 37.6m [million] tonnes of petroleum products a year. The most productive oil crop that can be grown in this country is rape. The average yield is 3–3.5 tonnes per hectare. One tonne of rapeseed produces

415kg of biodiesel. So every hectare of arable land could provide 1.45 tonnes of transport fuel.

To run our cars and buses and lorries on biodiesel, in other words, would require 25.9m [million] hectares. There are 5.7m [million] in the UK. Even the EU's more modest target of 20% by 2020 would consume almost all our cropland.

If the same thing is to happen all over Europe, the impact on global food supply will be catastrophic: big enough to tip the global balance from net surplus to net deficit. If, as some environmentalists demand, it is to happen worldwide, then most of the arable surface of the planet will be deployed to produce food for cars, not people.

This prospect sounds, at first, ridiculous. Surely if there were unmet demand for food, the market would ensure that crops were used to feed people rather than vehicles? There is no basis for this assumption. The market responds to money, not need. People who own cars have more money than people at risk of starvation. In a contest between their demand for fuel and poor people's demand for food, the car-owners win every time. Something very much like this is happening already. Though 800 million people are permanently malnourished, the global increase in crop production is being used to feed animals: the number of livestock on earth has quintupled since 1950. The reason is that those who buy meat and dairy products have more purchasing power than those who buy only subsistence crops.

Creating an Environmental Disaster

Green fuel is not just a humanitarian disaster; it is also an environmental disaster. Those who worry about the scale and intensity of today's agriculture should consider what farming will look like when it is run by the oil industry. Moreover, if we try to develop a market for rapeseed biodiesel in Europe, it will immediately develop into a market for palm oil and soya oil. Oilpalm can produce four times as much biodiesel per hectare as rape, and it is grown in places where labour is cheap. Planting it is already one of the world's major causes of tropical forest destruction. Soya has a lower oil yield than rape, but the oil is a by-product of the manufacture of animal feed. A new market for it will stimulate an industry that has already destroyed most of Brazil's cerrado (one of the world's most biodiverse environments) and much of its rainforest.

It is shocking to see how narrow the focus of some environmentalists can be. At a meeting in Paris last month [October 2004], a group of scientists and greens studying abrupt climate change decided that [Great Britain's Prime Minister] Tony Blair's two big ideas—tackling global warming and helping Africa—could both be met by turning Africa into a biofuel production zone. This strategy, according to its convenor,

"Washington DC . . . Republican Senators, Always Looking Out for America's Energy Needs," Cartoon by Chuck Asay. Copyright © 2005 Creators Syndicate, Inc. Reproduced by permission.

"provides a sustainable development path for the many African countries that can produce biofuels cheaply". I know the definition of sustainable development has been changing, but I wasn't aware that it now encompasses mass starvation and the eradication of tropical forests. Last year [2005], the British parliamentary committee on environment, food and rural affairs, which is supposed to specialise in joined-up thinking, examined every possible consequence of biofuel production—from rural incomes to skylark numbers—except the impact on food supply.

We need a solution to the global warming caused by cars, but this isn't it. If the production of biofuels is big enough to affect climate change, it will be big enough to cause global starvation.

Increasing the Use of Biofuels Could Eradicate Hunger Worldwide

United Nations Food and Agriculture Organization

This selection by the United Nations Food and Agriculture Organization (UNFAO), presented in April 2005 to the UN Committee on Agriculture, claims that biomass could benefit the estimated 2 billion people worldwide who still live without electricity. According to the FAO, increasing the use of bioenergy could enhance poor nations' agricultural output and guarantee such nations a cheap and steady source of energy. Developing bioenergy would also help poor countries raise their standard of living, thereby reducing poverty and hunger. The UNFAO heads international efforts to eradicate hunger. Serving both developed and developing countries, it acts as a neutral forum in which all nations meet as equals to negotiate agreements and debate policy.

Agriculture and forestry could become leading sources of bioenergy, a key element in achieving two of the UN [United Nations] Millenium Development Goals: eradicating extreme poverty and hunger and ensuring environmental sustainability, according to FAO [United Nations Food and Agriculture Organization].

A truck stuffed with sugar cane heads for a São Paulo ethanol plant. Brazil has benefited from fuel production using cheap, local sources.

In a paper presented to the nineteenth session of its Committee on Agriculture meeting, FAO recalls that around two billion people, mostly living in rural areas of developing countries, are still without electricity or other modern energy services.

Increased use of bioenergy can help diversify agricultural and forestry activities and improve food security, while contributing to sustainable development, the paper says.

Bioenergy is produced from biofuels (solid fuels, biogas, liquid fuels such as bioethanol and biodiesel) which come from crops such as sugar cane and beet, maize and energy grass or from fuelwood, charcoal, agricultural wastes and by-products, forestry residues, livestock manure, and others.

Biomass Reduces the Petroleum Import Bill

Biomass is a locally available energy source that can provide for heat and power. It contributes to the substitution of imported fossil fuels, thus enhancing national energy security, reducing the import bill of petroleum products and alleviating poverty.

FAO assists member countries in their interest to convert biomass into energy and set up national strategies and programmes. "The production and use of biofuels need to be properly managed in order to provide energy services to the rural poor while

An Indian villager chops wood for burning in a biomass power plant.

improving food security and contributing to sustainable development," explains FAO expert Gustavo Best.

In sub-Saharan Africa, where more than 90% of the rural population live without access to electricity, bioenergy—with its two main components, wood energy and agroenergy—can have a significant impact on improving livelihoods.

Improved Economic Development

Increasing the use of biomass for energy could lead to improved economic development, especially in rural areas, since it attracts investment in new business opportunities for small- and

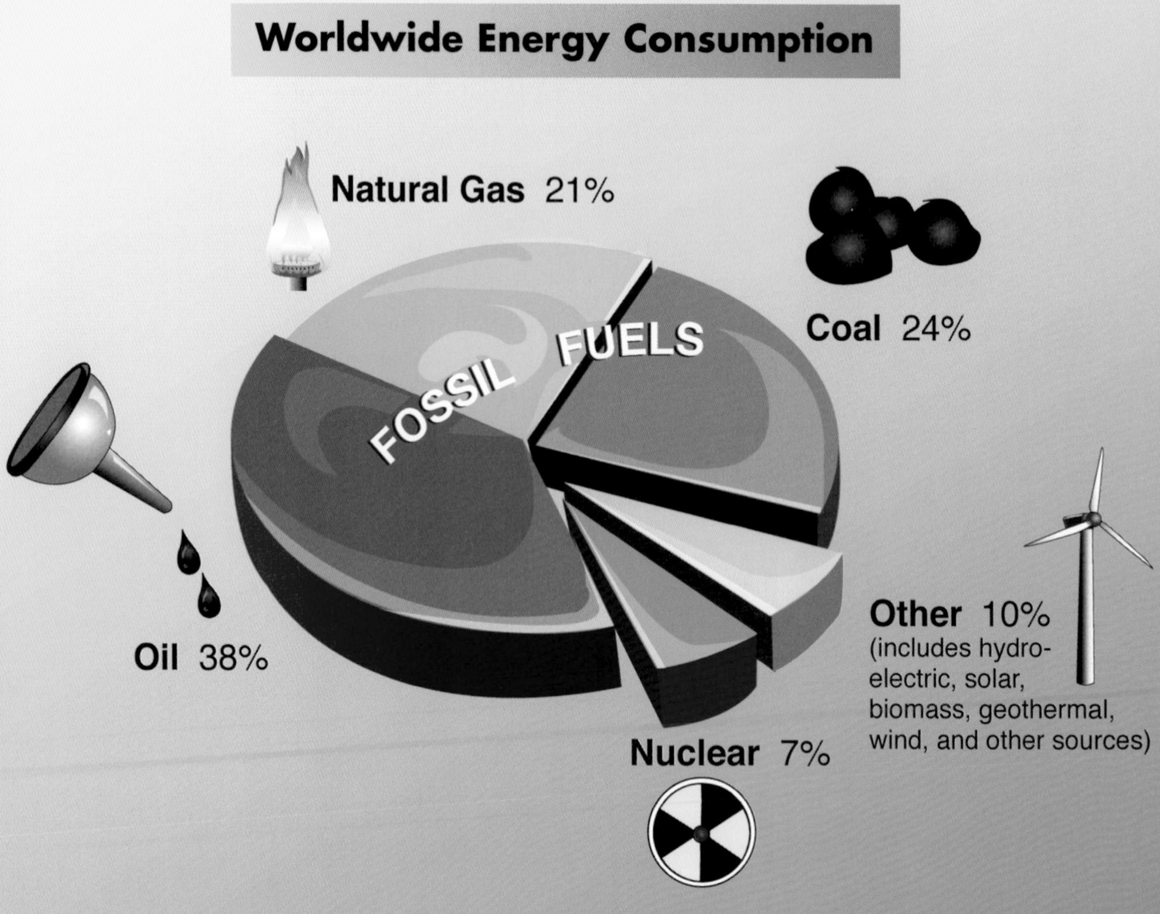

Worldwide Energy Consumption

Natural Gas 21%

Coal 24%

FOSSIL FUELS

Oil 38%

Other 10%
(includes hydro-electric, solar, biomass, geothermal, wind, and other sources)

Nuclear 7%

Source: Energy Information Administration, U.S. Department of Energy, 2005 (www.eia.doe.gov).

medium-sized enterprises in the field of biofuel production, preparation, transportation, trade and use.

The use of biomass for energy also generates incomes and jobs for the rural people. "In fact, bioelectricity production has the highest employment-creation potential among renewable energy options. It can create several times the number of direct jobs than the production of electricity using conventional energy sources, and with lower investment cost per job generated," the report says.

In developed countries, there is growing interest on the part of governments and the private sector in expanding the use of biofuels derived from agricultural and forestry biomass. Liquid biofuels have gained importance, particularly in the transport sector.

How America and Europe Can Use Biomass

Scenarios developed for the USA and the EU [European Union] indicate that "short-term targets of up to a 13% displacement of petroleum-based fuels with liquid biofuels (bioethanol and biodiesel) appear feasible on available cropland," according to FAO.

Petroleum accounts for over 35% of the world's total commercial primary energy consumption. Coal ranks second with 23% and natural gas third with 21%. These fossil fuels are the main sources of greenhouse gas emissions, causing global warming, and thus climate change, the report points out.

Biofuels, of which fuelwood and charcoal occupy the largest share, represent around 10% of the total global primary energy consumption.

For this century, the report anticipates a significant switch from a fossil fuel to a bioenergy-based economy which could benefit not only the rural poor but also the whole planet, since biofuels can help mitigate climate change.

The Use of Biomass Energy Harms the Environment

Forests.org

In the following selection, Forests.org argues that increasing the world's use of biomass for energy will harm the environment. According to the organization, forests and savannas are rapidly being cut down and cleared to make room for palm and soya crops, which are used to make biofuels. Forests.org recommends investment in solar and wind energy rather than in biomass. Forests.org is a project of the Ecological Internet, which uses the Internet to achieve conservation goals. Its mission is to empower the global movement for environmental sustainability by providing information retrieval tools, portal services, and analyses that aid in the conservation of ecosystems and help to jump-start their restoration.

To meet Kyoto protocol commitments [which call for a reduction in greenhouse gas emissions], various European and other governments are encouraging the use of biomass as fuel (biofuel) in transport and electricity. Indeed, dramatic climate change necessitates an embrace of renewable energy, and biofuel is an important and immediately available alternative energy. Biofuels are made from plant oils, crop wastes or wood, and can be used to run cars and power plants. They are mostly carbon neutral, as their burning returns to the atmosphere the carbon that the plants extracted during growth. Switching from

Forests.org, "Climate Conundrum as Biofuel Threatens Rainforests," http://www.climate ark.org, September 29, 2005. Reproduced by permission of Ecological Internet, Inc.

fossil fuels to biodiesel is promoted as a solution to climate change, but there exist serious concerns regarding biofuel's impacts upon tropical rainforests and land. . . .

There is only so much biomass and land available for biofuel production. Forests, and rainforests in particular, will most certainly be threatened by increased demand for agricultural products to be raised on once forested lands, and by use of forest biomass as a fuel. Throughout history agriculture has been a primary cause of deforestation as industries that covet forest land and fiber

A Brazilian farmer surveys damage to the rain forest that was burned to clear the land for farming. Some fear that more forests will be destroyed to make way for lucrative fuel crops.

inevitably overwhelm the resource base. An unregulated rush to biofuels will lead to more natural forest loss and fragmentation, increased pressures upon endangered primary forests, and more monoculture, herbicide laden and genetically modified tree plantations. Shifts from using limited lands to feed automobiles rather than people are also likely.

Palm and Soya Crops Are the Main Offenders

Two important tropical crops suitable as biofuels include palm oil, grown mostly in Southeast Asia, and soya from South America. Both are already grown for the food industry and enjoy

A Malaysian plantation worker stacks spiny palm-oil fruit, an important tropical oil fuel crop used to make biodiesel.

favorable prices, have existing markets and are otherwise economically attractive. Both are already amongst the world's major causes of tropical forest destruction, and further stimulation of the oil palm and soya markets for biofuel will surely result in massive new waves of irreversible destruction of tropical rainforests and savannas. Largely to meet demand for biofuel, the Indonesian government announced in July 2005 the development of the biggest palm oil plantation in the world which will clear the "Heart of Borneo", the vast areas of tropical rainforest in Kalimantan. This will further deteriorate habitat of the already endangered [orangutan], as well as many other species. Furthermore, the world production of soya is expected to nearly double by 2020, for which huge areas of tropical forests will disappear in Brazil, Argentina, Bolivia and Paraguay.

There exists an opportunity to influence European imports of oil palm in particular, as the European Commission is currently studying the matter. Palm oil is increasingly used by coal-fired power stations in the Netherlands, where it is heavily subsidized, and is also used in other European countries. Over the past nine years the Dutch import of palm oil from Indonesia has increased by 100% and from Malaysia a whopping 788% to 670,700 tons at present. It makes no sense to pursue modest improvements in climate change at the expense of the world's rainforests. The use of vegetable waste and regionally produced biomass is more appropriate. The world would be better off in pursuing energy conservation and truly renewable energy sources. Clearly the European Union and world should invest more strongly in energy from wind and sun, not in carelessly creating, stimulating and subsidizing new international palm oil and soy export markets.

The Use of Biomass Energy Benefits the Environment

Natural Resources Defense Council

In this selection the Natural Resources Defense Council (NRDC) discusses the environmental advantages of using biomass to make electricity, create heat, and power vehicles. The organization claims that the use of biomass energy produces no harmful sulfur emissions, while the carbon dioxide emitted can be used by plants, creating more biomass. Lower emissions, the NRDC points out, will reduce global warming. The NRDC is a prominent U.S. environmental action organization. It uses law, science, and the support of members and online activists to protect wildlife and wild lands in order to ensure a safe and healthy environment for all species.

Biomass energy uses organic matter such as wood or plants—called biomass—to create heat, generate electricity and produce fuel for cars that is dramatically cleaner than oil. Biomass energy is growing rapidly and now accounts for 45 percent of the renewable energy used in the United States. As its use expands, biomass helps America lower toxic pollutants in the air and decreases our reliance on foreign oil.

How It Works
Modern biomass energy recycles organic leftovers from forestry and agriculture, like corn stovers, rice husks, wood waste and

Natural Resources Defense Council, "Wind, Solar, Biomass Energy Today: Biomass Energy," www.nrdc.org, 2006. Copyright © 2006 Natural Resources Defense Council. Reproduced by permission.

pressed sugar cane, or uses special, fast-growing "energy crops" like willow and switchgrass, as fuel. These materials, called biomass, can be treated in different ways to produce electricity or clean-burning fuels for vehicles. Biomass can be:

- Burned like coal in power plants—but with fewer harmful emissions—to produce heat or electricity.
- Fermented to produce fuels, like ethanol, for cars and trucks.
- Digested by bacteria to create methane gas for powering turbines.
- Heated under special conditions, or "gasified," to break down into a clean-burning gas that can be used to make a range of products from diesel to gasoline to chemicals.

A tanker truck transports ethanol from a plant in Illinois. Biomass can generate electricity, create heat, or be processed to create ethanol.

The Carbon Cycle

Burning biomass (and other plant-based fuels like fossil fuels) creates CO_2 emissions. Because plants require CO_2 for growth, a carbon cycle is created when fuels made from plants are burned in power plants and vehicle engines.

Carbon Dioxide (CO_2)

Two oxygen molecules combine with one carbon molecule to form carbon dioxide.

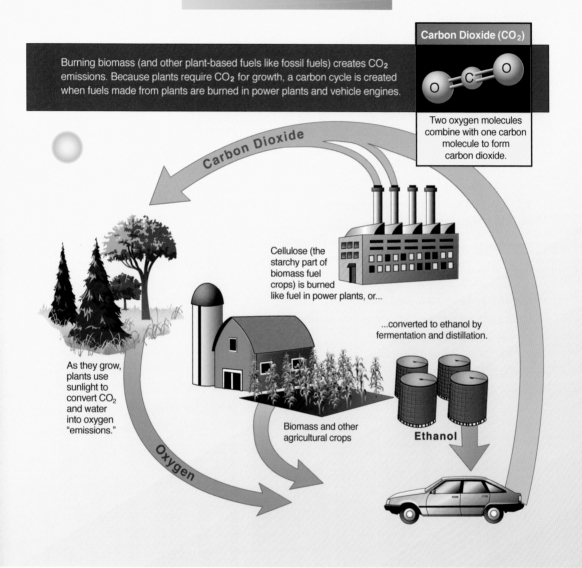

Carbon Dioxide

Cellulose (the starchy part of biomass fuel crops) is burned like fuel in power plants, or...

...converted to ethanol by fermentation and distillation.

As they grow, plants use sunlight to convert CO_2 and water into oxygen "emissions."

Biomass and other agricultural crops

Ethanol

Oxygen

Where It's Used

Most biomass in use today is burned for heat or used to make ethanol, but other, more efficient technologies are also being developed.

- Biomass power plants across the country burn agricultural waste to generate electricity for industries and residents. A biomass plant in Burlington, Vermont, for instance, uses wood waste to generate 50 megawatts of electricity annually, or enough to power more than 120,000 area homes.

- More than 100 biomass plants in 31 states burn methane gas generated from landfills.
- Some conventional power plants substitute biomass for a fraction of the coal they normally burn, reducing their sulfur dioxide and carbon dioxide emissions. When one medium-sized power plant adds biomass to its mix, its global warming emission reductions are equivalent to taking 17,000 cars off the road.
- In the Southeast and Pacific Northwest, the lumber, pulp and paper industries supply 60 percent of the energy they need to run their factories by burning wood waste.
- American farmers and refiners produce almost 4 billion gallons of ethanol a year from corn energy crops. There are currently 84 ethanol plants in the United States, and 16 more in the works. The ethanol they produce is usually blended with gasoline. All cars and trucks can use blends of 10 percent ethanol, and there are already nearly 5 million "flexible fuel" vehicles on the road that can use up to 85 percent ethanol.

> ## FACTS TO CONSIDER
>
> ### Biofuels Can Reduce Toxic Oil Spills
>
> Biofuels are essentially nontoxic and biodegrade readily. Every gallon of biofuels used reduces the hazard of toxic petroleum product spills from oil tankers and pipeline leaks (average of 12 million gallons per year, more than what spilled from the *Exxon Valdez*, according to the U.S. Department of Transportation). In addition, using biofuels reduces the risk of groundwater contamination from underground gasoline storage tanks . . . and runoff of vehicle engine oil and fuel.
>
> U.S. Department of Energy, "Environmental Benefits." http://eereweb.ee.doe.gov.

How Much It Costs

The cost of electricity from biomass energy depends on the type of biofuel used, how it's converted to electricity and the size of the plant. Power plants that burn biomass directly currently generate electricity at a cost of between 7 and 9 cents per kilowatt-hour.

Advantages

- There's plenty of biomass to go around, and we can keep growing more of it. Right now, roughly 39 million tons of crop residues go unused each year in the United States. If harnessed, this amount could produce about 7,500 megawatts of power—enough for every home in New England.

- Unlike coal, biomass produces no harmful sulfur emissions and has significantly less nitrogen, which means it cuts down on acid rain and smog.
- Burning biomass can result in zero net carbon dioxide emissions: any carbon dioxide released by burning biomass can be taken right back out of the atmosphere by growing more biomass.
- Using biofuels in our cars results in less global warming pollution than gasoline and allows us to invest our energy dollars at home instead of in foreign oil.
- Switchgrass, a promising source of biofuel, is a native, perennial prairie grass that is better for the environment than most row crops: it reduces erosion, produces very little nitrogen runoff and increases soil carbon. It also provides good wildlife habitat.
- About half of all ethanol production plants are owned by farmer-cooperatives, meaning that biofuels not only hold great promise for the environment, but are also helping to preserve the economic vitality of rural communities.

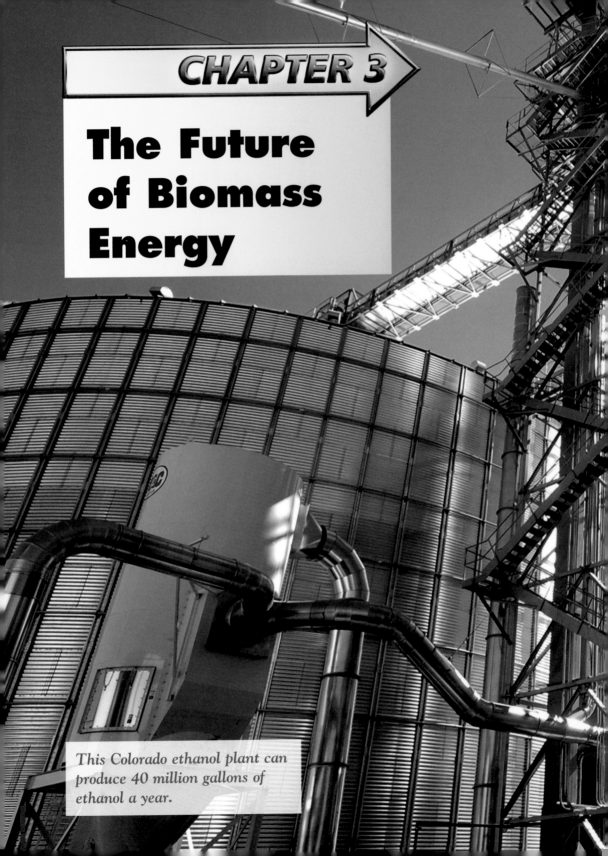

CHAPTER 3

The Future of Biomass Energy

This Colorado ethanol plant can produce 40 million gallons of ethanol a year.

Biomass Energy Will Reduce Dependence on Fossil Fuels

Amory B. Lovins and E. Kyle Datta

This excerpt from the 2004 book *Winning the Oil Endgame: Innovation for Profits, Jobs, and Security* focuses on the many specific ways in which biofuels could break America's reliance on oil. The authors argue that their strategy, which centers on replacing oil with biofuels, will both improve the national economy and help the environment. Amory B. Lovins, chief executive officer of the Rocky Mountain Institute (RMI), is a consultant experimental physicist. He has received the Right Livelihood ("Alternative Nobel"), World Technology, and TIME Hero for the Planet awards. E. Kyle Datta is senior director of RMI research and consulting. He is coauthor of RMI's influential, award-winning 2002 book *Small Is Profitable: The Hidden Economic Benefits of Making Electrical Resources the Right Size*. Datta is also president and founder of New Energy Partners, a renewable energy development company.

L iquid fuels made from farming and forestry wastes, or perhaps from energy crops, are normally considered to offer only a small potential at high cost. For example, classic ethanol production from corn, which now provides ethanol oxygenate equivalent to 2% of U.S. gasoline, could expand by only about half by 2025 if not subsidized. Modern production plants of this

Amory B. Lovins and E. Kyle Datta, *Winning the Oil Endgame: Innovation for Profits, Jobs, and Security*. Snowmass, CO: Rocky Mountain Institute, 2004. Copyright © 1999–2005. All rights reserved. Reproduced by permission.

type . . . yield net energy, but need favorable resale prices for their byproducts to compete with gasoline. And gasoline is already rather heavily subsidized.

Energy Times Are Changing

However, that widely held perspective . . . is outdated. When the National Academies' National Research Council found in a 1999 study that biofuels could profitably provide 1.6 Mbbl/d [million barrels per day] by 2020, new methods of converting cellulose- and lignin-rich (woody) materials into liquid fuels, e.g. using genetically engineered bacteria and enzymes, were just emerging. Five years later, even newer . . . technologies now permit biofuels by 2025 to provide 4.3 Mbbl/d of crude-oil equivalent at under $35/bbl ($0.75/gal gasoline-equivalent). . . .

Taking a global view, a 2004 IEA [International Energy Agency] biofuels report estimates that ". . . a third or more of road transportation fuels worldwide could be displaced by biofuels in

Genetically engineered enzymes (left) and bacteria (right) can help digest and ferment biomass cellulose.

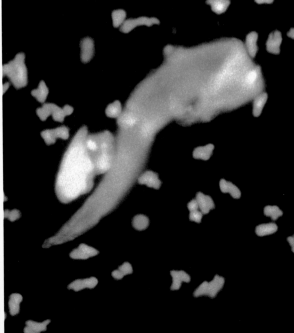

the 2050–2100 time frame." And a study for [U.S. Department of Defense] of how to relieve U.S. oil dependence . . . recommended a large-scale initiative in cellulosic biomass.

[As of 2004,] 99% [of the potential profit from biofuels] is from ethanol, largely from lignocellulosic feedstocks. The new technologies often use very efficient enzymes (many but not all from genetically modified bacteria, and the best about tenfold cheaper than they were two years ago) for both digesting cellulose and hemicellulose into sugars and then fermenting them. Other paths include thermal processes demonstrated at pilot-plant scale, such as the Pearson Gasification process, which produces Fischer-Tropsch ethanol from synthesis gas. (The F-T process connects small hydrocarbon molecules into long chains, produces a zero-sulfur and zero-aromatics synthetic diesel fuel completely compatible with existing infrastructure, and can be applied to syngas made from any hydrocarbon or carbohydrate.) Collectively, such innovations roughly double the yields, greatly reduce the energy inputs, and often reduce the capital costs of classical corn-ethanol processes. They also offer greater scope for coproducing valuable tailored biomaterials. The other 1% [of the profit] potential is biodiesel, an ester normally made by reacting an alcohol with vegetable oil; it too is becoming cheaper, and should soon compete in pretax price when using the cheaper kinds of feedstocks—especially those which, like used cooking oil, are often currently a disposal cost. Comparable bio-oils usable as diesel fuel can also be produced thermally from a wide range of feedstocks, . . . potentially increasing their fraction and the total size of the biofuel potential beyond that examined here. . . .

Other Countries Are Already Making Biofuels Work

Both ethanol and esterified biodiesel have been proven in widespread use, ethanol typically in 10–85% blends with gasoline and biodiesel in 2–100% blends with diesel oil. Brazil's 29-year-old ethanol program is now the world's low-cost producer. Using cheap sugar cane, mainly bagasse (cane-waste) for process heat and power, and modern equipment, it provides [approximately] 22% ethanol blend used nationwide, plus 100% hydrous ethanol

A car dealership employee polishes Volkswagen Total Flex vehicles which can run on gasoline, ethanol, or both.

for four million cars. The Brazilian ethanol program provided nearly 700,000 jobs in 2003, and cut 1975–2002 oil imports by a cumulative undiscounted total of $50 billion (2000 US$). . . .

The Brazilian government provided three important initial drivers: guaranteed purchases by the state-owned oil company Petrobras, low-interest loans for agro-industrial ethanol firms, and fixed gasoline and ethanol prices where hydrous ethanol sold for 59% of the government-set gasoline price at the pump. These pump-primers have made ethanol production competitive yet unsubsidized (partly because each tonne of cane processed can also yield [approximately] 100 [kilowatt-hours] of electricity via bagasse cogeneration—a national total of up to 35 billion [kilowatt-hours a year, approximately], 9% of national consumption).

In recent years, the Brazilian untaxed retail price of hydrous ethanol has been lower than that of gasoline per gallon. It has even been cheaper than gasoline—and has matched [the U.S.] 2025 cellulosic ethanol cost—on an energy-equivalent basis for some periods during 2002–04. Ethanol has thus replaced about one-fourth of Brazil's gasoline, using only 5% of the land in agricultural production. Brazilian "total flex" cars introduced by VW and GM in mid-2003 can use any pure or blended fuel from 100% gasoline to 100% ethanol, and are welcomed because they maximize customers' fuel choice and flexibility. (In contrast, the [approximately] 3 million "flex-fuel" vehicles now on U.S. roads, marketed partly to exploit a loophole in . . . efficiency standards but seldom actually fueled with ethanol, can't go beyond the "E85" blend of 85% ethanol with 15% gasoline.) . . .

In the U.S., the combination of vehicle efficiency and ethanol output analyzed here suggests that by 2025, the average light vehicle's fuel will contain at least two-fifths ethanol, rising thereafter—even more if ethanol is imported. To accommodate regional variations on this average, "flex-fuel" vehicles accepting at least E85 should therefore become the norm for all new light vehicles not long after 2010. "Total flex" vehicles like those now sold in Brazil would further increase the potential to accelerate ethanol adoption and to manage spot shortage of either gasoline or ethanol. In short, many of the fuel-system, commercial, vehicle-technology, and production developments that the U.S. would need for a large-scale biofuel program have already succeeded elsewhere; the main shift would be using modern U.S. cellulosic ethanol conversion technologies. . . .

Biofuels Offer Hope for the Environment

Since biofuels contain essentially no sulfur, trace metals, or aromatics, they also improve urban air quality, and can reduce CO_2 emissions by 78% for biodiesel or 68% for cellulosic ethanol. Properly grown feedstocks can even *reverse* CO_2 emissions by taking carbon out of the air and sequestering it in enriched topsoil whose improved tilth [condition] can boost agronomic yields. Using biofuels as a vehicle for better farm, range, and forest practices can also help to achieve other goals such as reduced soil erosion and improved water quality, and can dramatically improve the economies of rural areas. . . .

Fuel Emissions Comparisons

	Emissions from Ethanol E85 (85% ethanol and 15% gasoline) contain...
CO_2	35% to 80% less than 100% petroleum gasoline
NO_x	10% less than 100% petroleum gasoline
CO	Up to 40% less than 100% petroleum gasoline
Sulfates	80% fewer than 100% petroleum gasoline

	Emissions from 100% biodiesel contain...
Total Hydrocarbons	67% fewer than regular diesel fuel
NO_x	10% more than regular diesel fuel
CO	48% less than regular diesel fuel
Sulfates	100% fewer than regular diesel fuel

Carbon dioxide (CO_2) is a greenhouse gas; excess amounts in our atmosphere contribute to global warming.

Hydrocarbons and **nitrogen oxides (NO_x)** help form ozone and smog.

Carbon monoxide (CO) is a poisonous gas.

Sulfates are a major cause of acid rain pollution.

Sources: Argonne National Laboratory (www.anl.gov), U.S. Environmental Protection Agency (www.epa.gov), and Alternative Fuel Vehicle Institute (www.afvi.org).

Even without counting carbon and ecological benefits, biofuels' domestic and largely rural production could boost not just the national economy, but especially rural areas' economy, culture, and communities. An analysis of a proposal for 5-billion-gallon-a-year biofuel production by 2012 (1.8 times 2003 ethanol production) found that cumulatively through 2012, it could save a total of 1.6 billion barrels of oil, cut the trade deficit by $34 billion, generate $5 billion of new investment and 214,000 new jobs, boost farm income by $39 billion, and save $11 billion of farm subsidies. Similar benefits are becoming apparent in Europe, whose 430 million gallons of biodiesel production in 2003 (vs. 25 in the U.S.) won support from both oil and auto companies as well as from farmers and those wishing to reduce farmers' costly surpluses and subsidies to conform to the 1 August 2004 world trade agreement.

Biofuels Will Benefit Farmers

U.S. Department of Energy

According to the U.S. Department of Energy's Office of Energy Efficiency and Renewable Energy (EERE), farmers who grow crops to make biofuels can realize increased profits. Farmers growing corn for producing ethanol have already benefited, the agency claims, and those who invest now in crops for biodiesel will reap advantages in the future. Moreover, farmers can feel good about reducing the nation's dependence on foreign sources of oil and improving the environment by investing in clean, renewable biofuels. The EERE's Biomass Program develops technology for the conversion of biomass (plant-derived material) to valuable fuels, chemicals, materials, and power, trying to reduce dependence on foreign oil and foster growth of biorefineries.

A merican farmers have a great opportunity, now and in the coming years, to help make the nation more self-sufficient in energy, and to reduce air pollution, including emissions of "greenhouse gases". Advances in technologies for making "biofuels" like ethanol and biodiesel mean that new markets are opening up. These can provide extra farm income, help to revitalize rural communities, and improve the environment at the same time. Corn ethanol has been around since the 1970s, but national production is going up fast and costs are coming down—and now there are new ways to make ethanol from a variety of agricultural raw materials, as well as growing markets for other biofuels like biodiesel.

U.S. Department of Energy, Oak Ridge National Laboratory, "Biofuels and Agriculture: A Factsheet for Farmers," www.eere.gov, September 2001. Reproduced by permission.

New and Old Materials for Making Biofuels

A range of raw materials are available, some already in use and others which will supplement them in the near-term and longer-term future. For example, fuel ethanol is currently produced from the easily fermented sugars and starches in grain and food processing wastes. Biodiesel is made from oil-seed crops such as soybean and canola.

Soon, new technologies will be economically viable for converting plant fiber to ethanol. A portion of the agricultural and forestry residues (stalks, leaves, branches) which are presently burned or left in the field may therefore be harvested for biofuel production. Residues such as corn stover [the plants' stalks and leaves] may represent a very large resource—over 100 million tons

An Oregon power company worker tosses tree trimmings into a chipper. Forestry waste is commonly used in biofuel production.

nationwide. The U.S. Departments of Energy and Agriculture are cooperating on research to determine how much corn stover can be removed sustainably.

New crops may be grown specifically for biofuel production, including native grasses and trees, as well as new high-yielding varieties of oil-seed crops. In time, these energy crops may be planted in place of millions of acres of surplus arable crops, surpassing even corn stover as an energy resource. Switchgrass is a high-yielding perennial grass that grows well over most of the central and eastern United States. Fast-growing trees, which are usually harvested every 3–10 years and can be harvested repeatedly, include poplar and willow in cooler regions, and sycamore and sweetgum in warmer regions.

The Ethanol Industry

The ethanol industry currently employs about 200,000 people (directly and indirectly), and saves $2 billion a year in terms of oil imports. However, America's present trade deficit in crude oil is over $50 billion, so there is plenty of room for growth. Ethanol's total benefits in terms of farm incomes are greater—about $4.5 billion. There are over 60 ethanol production plants in operation or under construction, with the capacity to produce more than 2 billion gallons (7.6 billion liters) a year. Ethanol plants are found in 20 states, mostly concentrated in the corn-growing region of the Midwest. 22 of these plants are farmer-owned facilities, representing one-quarter of total capacity.

Future Market Potential

Today, about 12% of US gasoline contains ethanol as a fuel additive, which boosts octane and reduces carbon monoxide and other emissions. Another 25% of US gasoline contains an additive called MTBE which has caused concerns about water pollution. State legislation in California and nine other states to ban MTBE in reformulated gasoline is likely to generate a significant new demand for ethanol. USDA [U.S. Department of Agriculture] has estimated that this would result in an extra $1 billion in farm cash receipts annually, while ethanol produc-

Growth in U.S. Ethanol Production

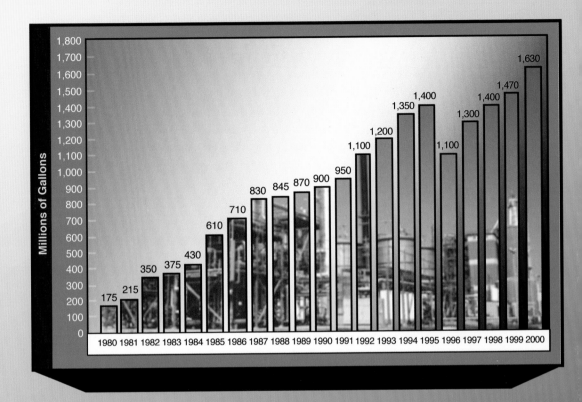

Sources: Energy Information Administration/Renewable Fuels Association.

tion could more than double within the next 5 years. An estimated one billion gallons of new ethanol production capacity is already on the drawing board, about 35% of this based on non-grain feedstocks such as agricultural and forestry residues. Doubling ethanol production would create a demand for an additional 800 million bushels of corn, or 20–25,000 tons of corn stover, other residues, or switchgrass.

Corn Stover

With good planning and sufficient research and development, the first commercial plants producing ethanol from stover could begin operation as early as 2010. However, there are important reasons for farmers to be thinking about collecting stover today. Depending on your own particular conditions, this may require significant changes to your harvesting and tilling practices. Some small-scale markets for stover already exist, e.g. mulch production, so it may be worth while experimenting with an eye to future markets. Farmers are likely to play a key role in making cellulose-to-ethanol technology a success. For obvious reasons, corn stover is already available in the same areas where corn-to-ethanol plants are located, and this may enable the development of more cooperatively-owned ethanol plants.

Ethanol can be created from corn kernels, stalks, husks, and other plant material left over after the harvest.

Biodiesel Production

The biodiesel industry is much smaller, but growing fast. Enabling legislation to promote biodiesel use is advancing rapidly, and more state and federal vehicle fleets (e.g. the U.S. Postal Service) are starting to use this fuel. About 20 million gallons (76 million liters) of biodiesel were actually produced in 2001, but U.S. capacity is already 50 million gallons (190 million liters) per year, and growing.

Biodiesel can now be used in blends of 20% and higher to meet federal and state alternative fuel vehicle fleet requirements, due to legislation under the Energy Policy Act. A number of city bus fleets, such as Cincinnati and St. Louis, are beginning to use biodiesel on a large scale, and legislation requiring statewide use of a 2% biodiesel blend has been proposed by the legislatures of Minnesota and North Dakota. These two states alone would create a market for 20 million gallons (76 million liters) per year. The ultimate market for biodiesel over the next few years could reach as much as 2 billion gallons (7.6 billion liters) per year, or about 8% of highway diesel consumption.

Overall Economic Benefits

Establishment of major new biofuel industries in rural areas is likely to have substantial economic impacts. Preliminary estimates by Oak Ridge National Laboratory suggest that ethanol production from corn stover alone could result in $8.9 billion in industrial output and $3.8 billion in value added, creating about 76,000 permanent jobs. Another study, for switchgrass production, found that total US farm income could increase by $6 billion. At the local level, a USDA study estimated that a 100 million gallons/year (380 million liters/year) ethanol production facility would create 2,250 local jobs for a single community. The National Biodiesel Board estimates that inclusion of just 1% biodiesel (partly replacing sulfur as a lubricity additive) in all road diesel fuel would generate demand for 300 million gallons (1.1 billion liters) of biodiesel adding more than $800 million to gross farm incomes.

Environmental Benefits

Biofuels, when blended with conventional fuels, reduce air pollutant emissions such as sulfur, particulates, carbon monoxide and hydrocarbons. Ethanol and biodiesel are also less of a hazard if they spill or leak, since they are rapidly biodegradeable in water. Substituting biofuels for one gallon of gasoline or diesel saves up to 20 pounds of carbon dioxide emissions to the atmosphere, since they are made from carbon "recycled" by plants instead of carbon dug out of the ground in the form of fossil fuels.

Growing perennial energy crops in place of surplus annual crops can reduce soil erosion and compaction, as permanent deep root systems develop and enrich the soil. Perennial crops need less tilling and less agrochemical inputs, so they may help to improve the quality of waterways. Their sturdy root systems and more permanent canopies offer a wider variety of habitats for birds and beneficial insects, compared with annual row crops. Levels of soil carbon may increase under perennial crops, helping to offset some fossil-fuel carbon dioxide emissions. Soil carbon sequestration may even occur under intensively-managed annual crops with limited residue removal, such as the harvest of about half the available corn stover. However, the optimal sustainable level of stover removal will depend on many factors, including erosion control, moisture retention and planned tillage reduction, and will be highly specific to local conditions and topography.

In the future, there may even be financial opportunities for farmers through rewards for good stewardship of the land in terms of "carbon credits". A number of US electricity utilities are already showing an interest in future trading of carbon emissions and offsets.

Great Times Ahead for Biofuels

So next time you hear your neighbors complaining about fuel prices, tell them what U.S. farmers can do! American agriculture can help not only to reduce our dependence on imported oil—a growing domestic biofuels industry will also assist in ironing out the ups and downs of energy costs, and can also contribute to storing carbon in the soil. In a few years your neighbors will probably be using biofuels themselves, or will know someone who does!

Microbes Could Make Ethanol Production Easier

Paul Elias

Paul Elias explains in this article how scientists are researching the use of microbes to break down massive amounts of biomass quickly, easily, and inexpensively. In contrast to current methods of making ethanol, which some scientists argue use more energy than they produce, using microbes can do the job on a much bigger scale and thus save energy. Elias mentions that scientists hope to create completely new lifeforms that would have the enzymes necessary to eliminate several steps in the biomass-to-biofuel creation process. Paul Elias is a biotechnology writer for the Associated Press.

The key to kicking what President [George W.] Bush calls the nation's oil addiction could very well lie in termite guts, canvas-eating jungle bugs and other microbes genetically engineered to spew enzymes that turn waste into fuel.

It may seem hard to believe that microscopic bugs usually viewed as destructive pests can be so productive. But scientists and several companies are working with the creatures to convert wood, corn stalks and other plant waste into sugars that are easily brewed into ethanol.

Scientists Say It Can Happen Now

Thanks to biotechnology breakthroughs, supporters of alternative energy sources say that after decades of unfulfilled promise

Paul Elias, "Researchers Seeking Cheap Way to Produce Ethanol: Microbes May Allow the Alternative Fuel to Be Made in Big Quantities From Farm Wastes," *Los Angeles Times*, February 13, 2006. Reproduced by permission of the Associated Press.

and billions in government corn subsidies, energy companies may be able to produce ethanol easily and inexpensively.

"The process is like making grain alcohol, or brewing beer, but on a much bigger scale," said Nathanael Greene, a Natural Resources Defense Council analyst. "The technologies are out there to do this, but we need to convince the public this is real and not just a science project."

Using microbes may even solve a growing dilemma over the current ethanol manufacturing process, which relies almost exclusively on corn kernels and yielded only 4 billion gallons of ethanol last year [2005] (compared with the 140 billion gallons of gasoline used in the U.S.). There's growing concern in the Midwest that the 95 ethanol plants are increasingly poaching corn meant for the dinner table or livestock feed.

A trucker unloads corn at an Iowa ethanol plant. New technologies may make the biomass-to-fuel process easier and less expensive.

The idea mentioned by Bush during his [2006] State of the Union speech—called "cellulosic ethanol"—skirts that problem because it makes fuel from farm waste such as straw, corn stalks and other inedible agricultural leftovers.

Breaking cellulose into sugar to spin straw into ethanol has been studied for at least 50 years. But the technological hurdles and costs have been so daunting that most ethanol producers have relied on heavy government subsidies to squeeze fuel from corn.

Tiny Life Forms Could Make the Dream a Reality

Researchers are now exploring various ways to exploit microbes, the one-cell creatures that serve as the first link of life's food chain. One company uses the microbe itself to make ethanol. Others are taking the genes that make the waste-to-fuel enzymes and splicing them into common bacteria. What's more, a new breed of "synthetic biologists" are trying to produce the necessary enzymes by creating entirely new life forms through DNA.

Bush's endorsement of the waste-to-energy technology has renewed interest in actually supplanting fossil fuels as a dominant energy source—a goal long dismissed as a pipe dream.

"We have been at this for 25 years, and we had hoped to be in commercial production by now," said Jeff Passmore, an executive vice president at ethanol maker Iogen Corp. "What the president has done is—perhaps—put some wind in the sails."

Ottawa-based Iogen is already producing ethanol by exploiting the destructive nature of the fungus *Trichoderma reesei*, which caused the "jungle rot" of tents and uniforms in the Pacific during World War II.

Through a genetic modification known as directed evolution, Iogen has souped up fungus microbes so they spew copious amounts of digestive enzymes to break down straw into sugars. From there, a simple fermentation—which brewers have been doing for centuries—turns sugar into alcohol.

Expanding Research into Enzymes

Although no commercial interest has advanced as far as Iogen, other biotech companies are engineering bacteria to spit out

Researchers pose with fermenters containing the T. reesei enzyme. The inset photo shows a closeup of the frothy biomass mixture.

similar sugar-converting enzymes, and academics are pursuing more far-out sources.

At Caltech, Jared Leadbetter is mining the guts of termites for possible tools to turn wood chips into ethanol. Leadbetter said there are some 200 microbes that live in termite bellies that help the household pest convert wood to energy.

Those microbes or their genetic material can be used to produce ethanol-making enzymes. So scientists at the Energy Department's Joint Genome Institute in Walnut Creek, Calif., are now sequencing the microbe genes in hopes of finding a key to ethanol production.

Burning Landfill Gas for Energy Can Reduce Global Warming

Natural Resources Defense Council

According to the Natural Resources Defense Council (NRDC) in this selection, burning the gas produced when organic matter in landfills decomposes instead of allowing it to escape would reduce dangerous emissions. Although burning landfill gas for energy produces carbon dioxide, this substance is far less dangerous than the methane normally allowed into the atmosphere at most landfills, the organization maintains. The NRDC believes that landfills in general harm the environment, but it points out that using methane to produce energy mitigates landfills' negative effects. The NRDC's philosophy is to use law, science, and the support of its many members and online activists to protect the planet's wildlife and wild places in order to ensure a safe and healthy environment for all living things.

Municipal solid waste landfills, long reviled by the environmental community as sources of air and water pollution, have in recent years benefited from numerous subsidies associated with alternative fuels and renewable power. Federal and state tax credits and payments are now offered to landfill facilities that collect and utilize landfill gas for heat or electricity generation.

Natural Resources Defense Council, "Is Landfill Gas Green Energy?" www.nrdc.org, February 7, 2006. Reproduced by permission.

Three related concerns have been raised with regard to these incentives. First, some have raised concerns about the health impacts of the exhaust from burning landfill gas. Second, some have pointed to the substantial environmental and public health damage caused by landfills and called into question the sustainability of landfills themselves and thus landfill gas. Finally, some have suggested that these subsidies are just another stone on the scale promoting landfilling over recycling.

A trash truck dumps garbage into a landfill. The methane-rich gas generated by landfills can be used as a biomass energy source.

What Is Landfill Gas?

The United States generated 231.9 million tons of municipal solid waste (MSW) in 2000, 55 percent of which ended up in the country's 2000 landfills. Landfill gas (LFG) is naturally produced by the decomposition of organic materials (also known as biomass) in landfills, and approximately 60 percent of the non-recovered MSW is organic. Landfill gas contains mostly methane and carbon dioxide, both of which are greenhouse gases that contribute to global warming. Methane, which comprises about 55 percent of LFG, has 23 times the global warming potential of carbon dioxide, and although its worldwide emissions are much smaller than those of carbon dioxide, methane's potency as a greenhouse gas has marked it as the second most important anthropogenic (originating from human activity) greenhouse gas. In addition, LFG may contain small but significant amounts of ozone-forming volatile organic compounds (VOCs) and toxic or carcinogenic hazardous air pollutants (HAPs).

Landfill gas is a threat to human health and global warming, and flaring or utilizing it for energy greatly reduces its climate change impact. Burning LFG also serves to mitigate its public health impact by destroying the majority of hazardous air pollutants in landfill gas through the combustion process. Furthermore, using LFG to produce electricity avoids the need to generate electricity at traditional power plants and thus reduces air pollution from these plants. However, LFG combustion produces minute quantities of dioxins, an extremely toxic group of chemicals that are harmful even in very small amounts. . . .

Since the cost-effectiveness of recycling programs is directly linked to the cost of alternative waste-management options, landfill-gas energy (LFGE) subsidies could possibly reduce the competitiveness of recycling programs by enabling landfill operators to charge lower tipping fees. Each LFGE project is uniquely affected by LFGE incentives. Some projects may depend on subsidies to break even, while others may be cost-effective even without subsidization. . . . In drawing our conclusions on [the merits of using landfill gas for energy] and laying out the policy guidance that follows from these conclusions, we have tried to balance idealism and reality. As Allen Hershkowitz wrote in his wonderful book, *Bronx Ecology:* "To truly deliver tangible ecological benefits to the world, environmentalists must emphasize a practical side to idealism."

The Harms and Benefits of Landfill Gas

- Combustion of raw LFG in a flare, an engine, or a turbine dramatically reduces the overall toxicity. Raw LFG contains many hazardous air pollutants, many of which are carcinogenic. The destruction of the vast majority of these more than makes up for the formation of minute amounts of dioxins. Our analysis of the inhalation cancer-risk factor suggests that the overall toxicity of LFG combustion is 23 times less than that of raw LFG.
- Collection and combustion dramatically reduce global warming impacts and toxicity. As mentioned above, LFG contains a lot of methane and methane is a very powerful heat-trapping gas. The combustion of LFG converts the methane to carbon dioxide, which while still a heat-trapping gas, is dramatically less powerful.
- Using LFG to generate electricity further reduces the greenhouse gas impacts and also reduces emissions of nitrogen oxides, sulfur dioxide and mercury. By displacing demand for electricity from traditional power plants, LFGE projects further reduce these important pollutants. However, when LFG is already being flared, the emission reductions are substantially less. Furthermore much depends on exactly what type of power plant is being displaced. If new natural-gas power plants or renewables are being displaced, then LFG may be better off simply flared.
- Burying garbage in landfills results in the release of more heat-trapping gases than any other waste-management option. The best way to combat LFG is to avoid landfilling biomass. This is true regardless of how much LFG is collected and used for energy. The best strategies are resource reduction and recycling.
- Because LFG is a by-product of landfills, and landfills are such a poor way to manage our waste, LFG can not be considered

renewable. In addition to the global warming impacts of landfills, they are also a source of groundwater pollution. At best, the Environmental Protection Agency's (EPA) current landfill regulations merely postpone the inevitable damage landfills will cause. Landfills are simply unsustainable, and therefore so is LFG.

A utility worker checks a landfill gas-extraction system.

Recommendations Concerning Landfill Gas

Based on these findings, we can establish the following hierarchy of priorities:

1. Avoid LFG by avoiding landfills. The first priority must be increased resource reduction and recycling. Biomass—especially paper—is easily recycled or composted. If there is no biomass in landfills, then there will be no LFG.

Electric transformers send power to thousands of homes surrounding a Washington landfill. Only a small percentage of U.S. landfill gas is captured and used for energy.

2. Burn all LFG that is produced. Even if we could close all landfills today, they would continue to produce LFG for years to come. Combusting LFG in an engine, a turbine, or simply in a flare has tremendous benefits in terms of reduced toxicity and reduced greenhouse gases. Sixty one percent of LFG is generated at landfills with no collection system and at least 25 percent of LFG at landfills with collection systems simply escapes. Collecting all of this gas and burning it—preferably for energy, but at least in a flare—should be a priority nearly equal to avoiding landfills.

3. Use LFG for energy production. While there are instances where the use of LFG for energy can increase the amount of certain pollutants, the balance of benefits is in favor of using LFG for energy. Generally turbines are cleaner than engines, though less efficient. However, the benefits of LFGE are greatest if we also increase air pollution regulations and energy efficiency so that we displace coal plants instead of gas plants.

Facts About Biomass

Sources of Biomass Fuels
- Biomass is plant or animal matter. Biomass fuels are created from alcohol fuels (by fermenting crops such as corn, sugar beets, or grasses, or by fermenting by-products of cheese and paper manufacturing), wood, agricultural wastes (stalks, husks, prunings, straw, and corn cobs), animal wastes, and municipal solid waste (which produces usable gases called landfill gases).
- Cellulosic biomass consists of tree trimmings, logging slash, crop residues, and organic matter that might otherwise go to landfills. It also consists of the wood residue of forest product mills, such as sawdust, bark, and woodchips.
- Cellulosic ethanol is considered superior to corn ethanol because it takes less energy to produce and emits fewer greenhouse gases in the production process.
- Every year, plant biomass captures energy equivalent to about eight times the total energy in all forms (including oil, coal, natural gas, wind, and hydro) used by people.

Measuring Biomass Energy
The energy content of biomass fuels is measured in Btus (British thermal units). The energy produced by a lit match is approximately one Btu.

Biomass Energy Benefits
- Using more biomass would reduce sulfur dioxide, carbon, nitrogen oxide, and methane emissions.
- Using biomass such as tree trimmings would reduce the amount of refuse sent to landfills.
- Biomass fuels are nontoxic and biodegradable.
- Increased biomass use would cut down on the use of fossil fuels, thereby reducing damaging oil spills and pipeline leaks.
- Thinning forests to obtain biomass fuel would reduce the risk of wildfires.

- While the burning of biomass does create carbon dioxide, when the biomass originally grows, it absorbs carbon dioxide, thus making biomass carbon neutral. Some scientists believe this characteristic of biomass makes it an ideal energy source for reducing the global warming caused by greenhouse gas emissions.
- Enlarging the biomass industry would create jobs.

Biomass Energy Drawbacks

- Biomass produces what many scientists call net negative energy; that is, the total energy produced is usually less than the energy used to make biomass-based fuels, considering the energy needed to grow, harvest, produce, and transport biomass.
- Growing only one or two biomass crops for energy would reduce overall biological diversity.
- Biomass crops only grow part of the year, and they may die due to drought, disease, or insect infestation before they can be harvested.
- Burning agricultural wastes instead of plowing them back into fields may deprive the soil of nutrients.
- Burning municipal solid waste may release toxic emissions.
- Harvesting large areas of land to produce biomass fuels can damage wildlife habitats and cause erosion.
- Using crops to produce alcohol fuels may take away from their use as food.
- Large amounts of energy are often needed to harvest and transport crops long distances.

Methods of Biomass Fuel Production

- **pyrolysis:** Heats biomass with no oxygen, producing char, liquid oil, and a combustible gas.
- **hydrolysis:** Breaks down the tougher parts of plants through "steam explosion" of cell walls or dissolving with acids, enzymes, or organic solvents. The resulting sugars are then converted into ethanol through fermentation using microbes.
- **direct combustion:** Generates electricity or heat energy by burning biomass in a boiler.

- **gasification:** Converts biomass to a combustible "producer gas" (carbon monoxide, methane, or hydrogen), which can be used to generate electricity, heat, and liquid fuels.
- **fermentation:** Changes plant starches to sugar and then ferments sugar into ethanol, which is then distilled. If cellulosic materials are used instead of traditional feedstocks (starch crops), the end product is bioethanol.
- **anaerobic digestion:** Causes bacterial decomposition of biomass into biogas (mostly methane and carbon dioxide).
- **transesterification:** A catalyst causes a chemical reaction that produces biodiesel (an ester made from fats or oils).

Biomass Production and Use Statistics

- In 2003 biomass was the leading source of renewable energy in the United States, providing 2.9 quadrillion Btus of energy. Biomass was the source of 47 percent of all renewable energy.
- Worldwide, biomass is the fourth-biggest energy resource after coal, oil, and natural gas. There are about 278 quadrillion Btus of installed biomass capacity worldwide. Most U.S. capacity is in the pulp and paper industries.
- About 2.5 billion people (a little less than half of Earth's population) are virtually dependent on traditional biomass use (in other words, the burning of wood and animal dung) for their cooking, heating, and lighting.
- About 18.4 gigawatts of biomass-fueled power generators were installed worldwide in developed countries in 2000, which is about 1 percent of total power generation capacities.
- As of 2006 all fifty U.S. states had at least one E85 (85 percent ethanol and 15 percent conventional gasoline) refueling station. E85 costs up to 35 percent less than gasoline. Much of this discount is from government subsidies and the elimination of the high taxes that normally apply to gasoline. However, that tax exemption is due to expire in 2007.
- In the United States biomass gasifiers have been developed and tested on a pilot and demonstration scale. On a two-hundred-megawatt-per-day scale, the Vermont Gasifier Demonstration Project has proven that quality fuel can be produced consistently from biomass.

- Pearson Technologies of Mississippi, Inc. has constructed a thirty-ton-per-day wood-waste-to-ethanol facility in Mississippi.

Future Developments in Biomass Technology

- By 2007 all new Brazilian cars are expected to be able to run on 100 percent ethanol. The nation's many biorefineries are fueled by locally grown sugarcane.
- Sweden has mandated that 60 percent of all large fueling stations must have an alternative fuel pump by 2009.
- The U.S. Department of Energy Biomass Program plans to complete a demonstrator integrated biorefinery by 2007. It also plans to help U.S. industry establish the first large-scale sugar biorefinery based on agricultural residues by 2010.
- An Indonesian plantation company, PT Bakrie Sumatera Plantations Tbk, is building a biodiesel plant that will come on line in mid-2008 and reduce the country's huge reliance on imported diesel.

Glossary

alternative fuels: Fuels or energy sources that can replace gasoline. Alternative fuels include compressed natural gas, alcohols, liquefied petroleum gas (LPG), and electricity.

anaerobic digester: A closed system without oxygen that uses natural microorganisms to produce methane and carbon dioxide from biomass. The methane can be burned as fuel or made into bioproducts and the leftovers used as fertilizer.

biodiesel: A fuel created by combining organically derived oils with alcohol (ethanol or methanol) and a catalyst to form ethyl or methyl esters. It can be made from soybean, canola, animal, waste vegetable, or microalgae oils. A simple chemical reaction removes the glycerin from the oil, leaving biodiesel behind. Biodiesel can be burned directly in any diesel engine or in most furnaces that burn heating oil.

biofuels: Short for "biomass fuel." The term refers to liquid fuels used for transportation such as ethanol and biodiesel.

biomass: All living matter is called biomass, but in discussions about energy, biomass refers to plant materials, animal wastes, and gases formed when the organic matter in landfills decays, all of which can be used as fuel. The chemical energy stored in this organic matter can be used to produce liquid fuels, electricity, heat, gaseous fuels, and useful chemicals.

biomass gasifier: A reactor that heats up biomass in a low-oxygen environment. It produces a gas that can fuel devices such as turbines and fuel cells, which generate electricity.

biorefinery: A facility that uses biomass conversion processes and equipment to produce power, fuels, and chemicals.

catalyst: A chemical substance that speeds up a chemical reaction without being consumed or changed. A catalyst can also cause the reaction to proceed at a lower temperature, saving energy.

cellulosic biomass: Energy crops grown specifically for fuel production. These materials have three major parts: cellulose, hemicellulose, and lignin. Cellulose and hemicellulose make up about two-thirds of biomass materials and can be fermented into ethanol. Lignin makes up most of the rest but cannot be fermented into ethanol.

energy crops: Plants grown for the specific purpose of producing liquid fuels or for burning in order to produce electricity. Switchgrass, willow, alfalfa, poplar, and eucalyptus are often grown as energy crops.

ethanol: The most widely used biofuel. It improves vehicle performance and reduces air pollution. Ethanol is an alcohol, and most is made using a fermentation process.

feedstocks: A biomass fuel resource. Some common sources are energy crops; forest, mill, and agricultural residues; animal manures; and urban wood wastes.

fermentation: A chemical reaction that converts carbohydrates, such as those in feedstocks, into alcohols or acids. Fermentation is a key process in the production of ethanol.

gasification: A process that converts carbon-containing materials such as biomass into hydrogen and carbon monoxide. These gases can be more easily changed into energy than burning the original form of fuel.

landfill gas: Carbon dioxide and methane produced by the decomposition of municipal solid waste by anaerobic microorganisms in sanitary landfills. The gases can be collected and burned to generate electricity or steam.

microbes: Microscopic living organisms such as viruses, bacteria, fungi, and protozoa. Some biomass-to-fuel conversion processes use chopped-up plants treated with enzymes. The enzymes break down complex plant molecules like cellulose into simple sugars, which microbes can then convert to ethanol.

municipal solid waste: Nonhazardous, unrecyclable garbage generated by businesses and households that typically ends up in a landfill.

oil crops: Plants that produce a lot of oil, like soybeans, sunflowers, rapeseed (canola), coconut, palm, and hemp. The oil-producing parts of the plant (usually the seeds) are harvested and then pressed to extract the oil. This oil can then be used for fuel.

renewable: A resource that can be replenished or replaced, either by human action or natural processes. Air, water, and forests are sometimes considered renewable. Biomass is a renewable resource.

starch crops: Starch crops such as potatoes, corn, and grains can be fermented to make ethanol, which can fuel gasoline engines the same way that vegetable oil fuels diesel engines.

sustainable: A process or practice that can continue indefinitely without creating a significant negative impact on the environment or its inhabitants.

thermochemical: A process in which solid biomass such as wood is converted to a gaseous or liquid fuel by heating it with oxygen. This increases burning efficiency and also allows the conversion of biomass to valuable chemicals or materials.

Chronology

1812
A London gas company demonstrates the first commercial use of pyrolysis, producing liquid oil from biomass.

1840
France builds the first commercial-scale biomass gasifier, a reactor that produces gas that can fuel devices such as turbines.

1860s
Wood is still the main fuel for heating and cooking in homes and businesses. Burning wood produces steam to run industrial processes, trains, and boats.

1870s
Gasifiers with engines begin generating power on a small scale.

1876
German scientist Nikolaus August Otto invents the first combustion engine (the "Otto Cycle") to use ethanol-blended gasoline.

1880s
American inventor Henry Ford uses ethanol to fuel the Quadricycle, one of his first automobiles.

1890
Despite technological advances in biomass technology, wood remains the primary fuel for residential, commercial, and transportation uses.

1900
German inventor Rudolf Diesel proves that his new engine can run on peanut oil.

1908
When designing the Model T, the first mass-marketed automobile, Henry Ford expects ethanol to be the fuel that runs it. He builds an ethanol fermentation plant in Atchison, Kansas.

1910s
Although wood is still widely used in rural North American homes, city residents begin to use coal for their energy needs.

1930s
Kerosene and fuel oil begin to overtake wood as people's primary energy source; ethanol fuels U.S. cars well into the 1920s and 1930s; by the 1930s over two thousand places in the Midwest sell "gasohol" (corn-derived ethanol).

1940s
With the influx of cheap, abundant petroleum after World War II, the U.S. ethanol fuel industry virtually shuts down.

1950
Electricity and natural gas heat most homes and commercial buildings in America.

1973
An oil embargo results in supply constrictions and steeply rising gas prices; throughout the 1970s concerns about oil shortages and environmental damage caused by the burning of fossil fuels spark new interest in ethanol and other biomass energy sources; many industrialized nations begin funding biomass research.

1974
Oil shortages cause a rise in woodstove sales for homes; the paper and pulp industries also install wood-fueled boilers for steam and power, displacing fuel oil and coal; oil companies market ethanol-blended fuels.

1978
Congress passes the U.S. Public Utility Regulatory Policies Act, which guarantees nonutility generators a market to sell power by mandating that utilities pay "avoided cost" (the utility's cost had it supplied the power itself) for the energy.

1984
Burlington Electric in Vermont builds a fifty-megawatt wood-fired plant for electricity production; in eastern Canada schools and large institutions modify heating systems to run on wood wastes.

1985

The fledgling California biomass power industry begins to grow, eventually adding 850 megawatts due to Standard Offer #4 contracts (ten-year guarantees of power prices).

1989

Canadian Solifuels, Inc. and Aerospace Research Corporation try direct-wood-fired gas turbine plants for the first time.

1990

U.S. electricity generation from the nation's 190 biomass-fired facilities reaches six gigawatts (excluding municipal solid waste facilities); the U.S. Clean Air Act mandates the sale of oxygenated fuels (such as ethanol-blended gasoline) in polluted cities; European nations spur the use of biodiesel fuels; the United Nations reports that biomass energy provides 6.7 percent of total global energy consumption.

1992

The pioneering California biomass industry overbuilds, causing biomass fuel resource prices to reach a high of fifty-five dollars per dry ton as the last of the Standard Offer #4 contract power plants come on line; new biomass sources eventually lower costs to about thirty-five dollars; Canada grants a tax exemption for use of ethanol-blended fuels.

1994

Several biomass gasification tests identify hot gas cleanup as key to widespread adoption of the technology.

1995

Half of the California biomass power industry shuts down; by August, fifteen biomass power plants (with a total of 500 megawatts of capacity) were closed through sales or buyouts of their Standard Offer #4 agreements.

1998

With rising gas prices, shelved biomass research resumes, focusing on ways to reduce many countries' dependence on foreign supplies of oil.

2000

Congress passes the Biomass Research and Development Initiative; the International Energy Agency surveys 133 countries on energy use, reporting that the biomass share of total consumption is 10.5 percent.

2003

Ethanol production has grown from 175 million gallons in 1980 to 2.8 billion gallons.

2005

The Oak Ridge National Laboratory releases a report in April recommending that the U.S. bioenergy sector eventually take over 30 percent of total energy production; the report claims that such action would reduce dependence on fossil fuels, improve air quality, and create more rural jobs; the U.S. Energy Policy Act is signed into law in July, strengthening the ethanol industry and creating massive tax incentives for bioenergy use.

For Further Reading

Books and Papers

Chiras, Dan, *The Homeowner's Guide to Renewable Energy: Achieving Energy Independence Through Solar, Wind, Biomass, and Hydropower.* Gabriola Island, BC: New Society, 2006.

Estill, Lyle, *Biodiesel Power: The Passion, the People, and the Politics of the Next Renewable Fuel.* Gabriola Island, BC: New Society, 2006.

Lovins, Amory B., and E. Kyle Datta, *Winning the Oil Endgame: Innovation for Profits, Jobs, and Security.* Old Snowmass, CO: Rocky Mountain Institute, 2004.

Morris, Gregory, *Biomass Energy Production in California: The Case for a Biomass Policy Initiative,* Golden, CO: National Renewable Energy Laboratory, November 2000.

Pahl, Greg, *Biodiesel: Growing a New Energy Economy.* White River Junction, VT: Chelsea Green, 2005.

Tickell, Joshua, *Biodiesel America: How to Achieve Energy Security, Free America from Middle-East Oil Dependence, and Make Money Growing Fuel.* New York: Yorkshire, 2006.

Periodicals

Alternative Transportation Fuels Today, "ORNL Says Biomass Growth Could Prove Boon to Biofuels Sector," May 3, 2005.

Downing, M., T.A. Volk, and D. Schmidt, "Development of New Generation Cooperatives in Agriculture for Renewable Energy Research, Demonstration, and Development Projects," *Biomass and Bioenergy,* 2005.

Elias, Paul, "Researchers Seeking Cheap Way to Produce Ethanol," *Los Angeles Times*, February 13, 2006.

Fletcher, Anthony, "Palm Oil Demand Driving Orangutan to Extinction," *FoodNavigator-USA.com Newsletter*, September 23, 2005. www.foodnavigator-usa.com.

Keoleian, G.A., and T.A. Volk, "Renewable Energy from Willow Biomass Crops: Life Cycle Energy, Environmental, and Economic Performance," *Critical Reviews in Plant Sciences*, 2005.

Kidder, Norm, "Some Uses of Fire," *Bulletin of Primitive Technology*, 2001.

Koonin, Steven E., "Getting Serious About Biofuels," *Science*, January 27, 2006.

Monbiot, George, "Comment: Fuel for Nought," *Guardian*, November 23, 2004.

Novozyme and BBI International, "Fuel Ethanol: A Technological Evolution . . . an Industry Coming of Age," June 2005.

Pimentel, David, and Tad W. Patzek, "Ethanol Production Using Corn, Switchgrass, and Wood; Biodiesel Production Using Soybean and Sunflower," *Natural Resources Research*, March 2005.

UN Food and Agriculture Organization, "Bioenergy, Key to the Fight Against Hunger: Two Billion People Lack Access to Sustainable Energy Services," *FAO Newsroom*, April 14, 2005.

Web Sites

Biomass Research and Development Initiative (www.biomass.gov). Formed by the U.S. Biomass Research and Development Act of 2000, the Biomass Initiative is a multiagency effort to coordinate and accelerate bioenergy research and development. Its Web site provides information on the latest biomass technology and legislative updates.

Canadian Renewable Fuels Association (CRFA) (www.green fuels.org). Founded in 1994, the nonprofit CRFA works to promote renewable fuels for transportation through government liaison activities and consumer education. The Web site provides detailed information on ethanol and biodiesel, news about alternative energy, and event updates.

Centre for Energy (www.centreforenergy.com). The Centre for Energy was formed to provide credible, balanced information about the Canadian energy sector and energy-related issues. This Web site offers numerous resources on all matters relating to energy, including stock prices, compilations of the latest news from around the world, and numerous research links.

Climate Ark (www.climateark.org). Established as an online "climate change and global warming portal," Climate Ark promotes public policy that addresses global climate change through reductions in greenhouse gas emissions and deforestation, renewable energy, and energy conservation. Its Web site provides a wide range of information on all environmental topics.

Electrical Power Supply Association (ESPA) (www.epsa.org). Formed by a merger between the National Independent Energy Producers and the Electric Generation Association, EPSA's purpose is to give the competitive power supply industry a unified voice at the national level. Its Web site explains the organization's policy positions and provides the latest news on the electricity industry.

Energy Information Administration (www.eia.doe.gov). The EIA, created by Congress in 1977, is a statistical agency of the U.S. Department of Energy. It offers policy-independent data, forecasts, and analyses for policy making, and it works to assist public understanding of energy and its economic and environmental effects.

National Renewable Energy Laboratory (www.nrel.gov). Opened in 1974, the NREL is the principal research laboratory for the U.S. Department of Energy, Office of Energy Efficiency and Renewable Energy. This Web site compiles the latest news and much detailed information about alternative energy.

National Resources Defense Council (www.nrdc.org). The NRDC is an international environmental action organization. Its Web site has exhaustive information on major environmental issues and details efforts to expand the use of alternative energy sources such as biomass.

Oak Ridge National Laboratory (ORNL) (www.ornl.gov). The ORNL is the Department of Energy's largest science and energy laboratory. Its purpose is to conduct basic and applied research into new ways to solve complex problems. The lab's comprehensive Web site provides thorough information on the latest innovations in renewable energy.

Office of Energy Efficiency and Renewable Energy (EERE) (www.eere.energy.gov). The EERE Biomass Program, run by the U.S. Department of Energy, develops technology for converting biomass into valuable fuels, materials, chemicals, and power. This Web site offers extensive information on the biomass industry and the technology associated with it.

Renewable Energy Policy Project (REPP) (www.repp.org). Founded in 1995, REPP supports the advancement of renewable energy technology through policy research. Its Web site provides basic information on each kind of alternative fuel as well as links to energy policy news.

ScienceDaily.com (www.sciencedaily.com). An Internet portal for the latest research news, ScienceDaily.com's Web site features postings from numerous news outlets on everything related to science, from medicine to the environment.

Union of Concerned Scientists (UCS) (www.ucsusa.org). Founded in 1969 by Massachusetts Institute of Technology faculty members and students concerned about the misuse of science and technology, the UCS is an independent nonprofit alliance of more than one hundred thousand citizens and scientists. This Web site provides comprehensive analysis of and information on the environmental crises facing the planet.

Index

Picture Credits

Cover: AP/Wide World Photos
American Lung Association of Minnesota/U.S. Department of
    Energy/National Renewable Energy Laboratory, 49 (no. 8)
AP/Wide World Photos, 30, 33, 37, 81, 88, 96
Charles Bensinger/Renewable Energy Partners of New
    Mexico/U.S. Department of Energy/Renewable Energy
    Laboratory, 79 (both right)
Chip Somodevilla/Bloomberg News/Landov, 73
Getty Images, 14
© James Leynse/CORBIS, 95
Jay Mallin/Bloomberg News/Landov, 53
Jean-Pierre Pingoud/Bloomberg News/Landov, 60
© Kevin Fleming/CORBIS, 19
© Kim Komenich/San Francisco Chronicle/CORBIS, 69
Marcos Issa/Bloomberg News /Landov, 41
© The Mariners' Museum/CORBIS, 20
© Martin Bond/Photo Researchers, Inc., 24
Maury Aaseng, 27, 34, 38, 44, 49, 62, 70, 79, 83
Min Zhang/U.S. Department of Energy/National Renewable
    Energy Laboratory, 75 (right)
Neal Ulevich/Bloomberg News/Landov, 13
Nebraska Ethanol Board/U.S. Department of Energy/National
    Renewable Energy Laboratory, 83 (background)
Paul Roessler/U.S. Department of Energy/National Renewable
    Energy Laboratory, 27 (microalgae), 34 (background),
Paulo Fridman/Bloomberg News/Landov, 77
© Paulo Whitaker/CORBIS, 15
Photos.com, 23, 27 (all but microalgae), 43 (right), 54, 92
Reuters/Jayanta Shaw/Landov, 61
Russell Labounty/Ai Wire/Landov, 11
© Reuters/CORBIS, 50, 65
U.S. Department of Energy, 38 (background), 43 (left),
Warren Gretz/U.S. Department of Energy/National Renewable
    Energy Laboratory, 17, 34 (background), 49 (nos. 1–7), 75
    (both left), 79 (left), 84, 90 (both)
Zainal abd Halim/Reuters/Landov, 66

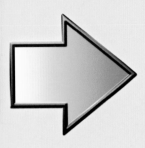

About the Editor

A member of the Board of Editors in the Life Sciences, Amanda de la Garza has been a freelance writer and editor since 1997. She is also a web designer and yoga instructor. Amanda lives with her husband and son on the Central Coast of California.